The Inner Loneliness

The Inner Loneliness

SEBASTIAN MOORE

CROSSROAD · NEW YORK

The Crossroad Publishing Company
575 Lexington Avenue, New York, N.Y. 10022

Printed in the United States of America

Library of Congress Cataloging in Publication Data

Moore, Sebastian, 1917–
The inner loneliness.

1. Loneliness—Religious aspects—Christianity.
2. Spiritual life—Catholic authors.   I. Title.
BV4911.M66   1982   248.4'82   82-14862
ISBN 0-8245-0515-8   0-8245-0619-7 pbk

For Tony,
and others of the new age

Acknowledgements

Thanks are due to the following for permission to reproduce copyright material:

The Confraternity of Christian Doctrine, Washington, D.C. for Scripture texts taken from THE NEW AMERICAN BIBLE © 1970. All rights reserved.

Viking Penguin Inc. 'The Gay Science' from *The Portable Nietzsche* tr. and ed. by Walter Kaufmann © 1954, The Viking Press Inc. © renewed 1982 by Viking Penguin Inc.

Contents

Introduction

The inner loneliness arises out of a paradox: that that in us which impels us to form relationships is, it seems, destined to be forever lonely. For that which impels me to form relationships and to embark on every other creative enterprise is the sense of myself as special, unique and without price; but no one can know me as I thus know myself, no one can touch me as I thus feel myself, no one can be present to me as I am thus present to myself. So there is a loneliness in each person that no other person can relieve.

As I think about myself and my life, my story, I form 'the idea of myself', not just my self-image but the very idea of 'me existing'. This idea intensifies my loneliness. Philosophy has endlessly tangled with it as 'the idea of being'. And it is not for nothing that the existentialism born of the tragic experience of two world wars centres on the image of the person as 'thrown into existence' and thus terribly and ineluctably alone as he or she looks out to the galaxies and the wastes of time.

The only companionship, then, that would dispel this otherwise ineluctable loneliness would be with one who *is* 'the idea of me existing', an unimaginable thought which is of me and of all that is (in all of which I am involved, and all of which is involved in me). As the idea of me by itself and with no point of reference but myself is the cause of a terrible loneliness, the *personhood* of this idea, could I but believe in it and be touched by it, would be the cause of a correspondingly devastating joy.

Now 'that which is the idea of me and of all, originally alive' is a tolerable paraphrase of Aquinas' favourite formula for God: *ipsum esse subsistens*, the *idea* of being, conscious, the idea as subject. And so we discover that this beautiful concept of the divine mystery behind our life is no longer confined to a medieval metaphysical matrix but describes the unconditionally desired of the human being. The Tillichian project of defining God by human need, which

1

Tillich never managed to equate, as to its term, with 'what all call God', can thus be carried through. To define God as the other within who dispels an otherwise ineluctable inner loneliness is to point to what Aquinas calls *ipsum esse subsistens*.

That is where I arrive in the first section of the first part of this book. In the second section I explore the human condition as we experience it, in which our self-love, far from regularly sending us out into creative and generous relationships and thus into the need for the transcendent partner, becomes disconnected from this self-gift which is the condition of its flourishing. The search for the cause of this disconnection takes me into the area of sexuality, where the tension between desire and control creates a cultural history of endless complexity: and at the root of it I discover a forlornness, the forlornness of being *constituted* a sexual being by a nature that is powerless to tell me who I am. Sexuality is the erotic experience of my enigmatic constitutedness. In other words, at the heart of men and women and of the whole history of men and women, there is a loneliness that all share and that therefore we cannot relieve in each other. *And we have met this before.* It is the inner loneliness, which we are now finding fleshed out in our existence as sexual beings. It is fleshed out, too, in the other two big areas of our world-constitutedness: our dependence on the planet for survival, and our mortality.

The second part of the book is a sustained contemplation of Jesus Christ as the one who dispels the inner loneliness and who, since God alone can perform this feat, is God. In him we see a new humanity, free of the inner loneliness, and consequently of its complicated sexual and other worldly implications. Spiritually free for the mystery that 'thinks' us, he is emotionally free for women and men, free of the anxiety that shapes our economics, and of the dread of death.

But for the imparting of this freedom to us we have to go beyond the sexual and economic experiences of the inner loneliness, to the most challenging of its three areas: death. Dying is the loneliest thing we shall ever do. So if our primordial desire for the partner who dispels the inner loneliness is to be satisfied, this must be as the crisis-point of our dying.

But here we meet a seemingly insurmountable difficulty. We have no experience of this final crisis-point. We do not know anyone who has died. Death is the jailer whose face we never see. Desire and death, it seems, never meet in us.

2

This brings me to the central idea of this book. Jesus awoke the primordial desire for the end of the inner loneliness, with a new and unique intensity. Sinless himself, he passed on the contagion of an unsuspected and impossible freedom. Now the *awakener* of this desire, by reason of the latter's uniqueness and of its being beyond the power of people to handle, becomes the *containing symbol* of the desire. So that when he is executed—and in a horrible way—*desire itself* comes into its mortal crisis for his followers. I suggest that this crisis of desire, experienced in the execution of a charismatic awakener of desire—and such are all great spiritual leaders—grounds the powerful sense we have, of the liberating, sacrificial significance of the leader's murder. Something of this sense was released with the assassination of Martin Luther King.

The followers of Jesus 'followed' him into a new dimension of human existence, that total desolation and emptying of the soul which alone ready it for the influx of God. And they experienced the influx. Jesus, alive beyond life and present to them, was its guarantee. The Spirit poured into them and uniting them was its divine energy. And millennia of recognition of the mystery behind life became spiritually constellated in the equation of this mystery with the loving parent of all existing.

In the third and last part, I embark on a new exploration. Touching again the mystery of our inner loneliness, I reflect upon the divine logos in us as response to 'the mystery that thinks us'. This reflection leads me to see the 'correspondence' between logos and God as strangely other than the correspondence, in the human mind, between the mind and its thought: the difference being that in God there is none of that surprise and subjection to reality without which human knowledge makes no real sense. In place of this surprise, this curiosity, there is that greatest of all divine mysteries, the Holy Spirit. Thus the doctrine of the Trinity begins to appear as the infinite structure of unloneliness.

Finally, I have to make an important, and sadly belated acknowledgement. The reader who has followed my christological inquiry through *No Exit*, *The Crucified Is No Stranger* and *The Fire and the Rose Are One* will observe in the latter work a marked change in direction. It was the decision to seek the original shape of Christian experience and faith primarily in the experience of the disciples of Jesus. It has been for me the most fruitful theological change of direction that I have ever made, so much so that I cannot now think of a Christology and a soteriology without it. It is far more thoroughly exploited in

3

this than in the preceding book. And the book that gave me the idea for it was Jon Sobrino's *Christology at the Crossroads*. The decision to recover theologically the experience of those whom Golgotha plunged into a terrible night of faith comes out of the contemporary Latin American experience. As opposed to a Christ whose victory is encapsulated in cult and in Caesarian church structures, the Catholic soul needs, in the dire circumstances of oppression, to enter into the oppressive situation out of which alone that victory came. So it seems I have plagiarized not only Sobrino but one of the generic sources of liberation theology, and indeed I am sorry. I can only point to that strange mechanical defect as a result of which important letters go unanswered and telephone calls unreturned.

PART ONE

Exploring the Inner Loneliness

Section One

What is self-awareness?

Self-awareness is what distinguishes the human from the other animals. But it is necessary to be very clear as to what we mean by 'self-awareness'. For the term easily suggests someone sitting down and wondering about himself, like the famous bronze nude of Rodin, 'The Thinker'. Or it suggests someone at a party nervously fingering his tie. Or it suggests a well-known moment comically described by Eliot in an early poem, 'Portrait of a Lady'.

I feel like one who smiles, and turning shall remark
Suddenly, his expression in a glass.

Now all these examples, and hundreds more you could come up with, are really descriptions not of self-awareness but of reflective self-awareness, or self-awareness intensified, and always distorted, by reflection.

Reflective self-awareness would not itself be possible were there not this prior condition of self-awareness *of which* it is the intensification and distortion.

Arguing with someone who insisted that we are only reflexively aware of ourselves, Lonergan asked, rather impishly, 'The self, of which you say you are not conscious until you reflect on it, is *that* conscious?' To say that we are not self-aware till we reflect is to think of 'the self' as being just like any other object you are not now thinking of, but may 'turn to'. But of course it's not. Turning to yourself, you do not meet a stranger. You intensify an act of self-awareness that was already going on; and which is going on in everybody all the time except for the periods of deep dreamless sleep. Outside those periods you are always consciously you, always you-ing.

The human action of transcending sensation is an act of self-awareness—very subtly so but really so. It is not merely that this power leads me to reflect on me its strange possessor. The very *exercise* of the power has 'me here' and 'all that I stand back from, there'. I am aware of myself as not immersed in pure sensation. Of course what I much more readily *notice* is what I *do* beyond pure sensation, such as summon the past to memory or the future to speculation, or summon the absent into my presence; but in all this, *I* am standing over my sensuous experience and able to judge it, I am behaving as a self behaves, and I am aware *in* this behavior. And this is what I mean by self-awareness.

When you point out to me something annoying that I frequently do, it does not come as a total surprise. If it did, if I had to take your description of my behaviour on faith, how could I correct my behaviour? I wouldn't know when the thing you are referring to was happening. But this is only one example of something that is observable throughout human experience. The self, aware, is self-aware. This is a very radical and challenging idea, and well worth spending some time on mastering.

To stop someone in the street is to break in on a sort of dialogue of the person with him or herself. You don't have to be wondering whether you will succeed in your job or arrive someplace on time to be 'in dialogue with yourself'. One is never totally *out of* dialogue except in deep dreamless sleep. We do not merely address people. We address their self-awareness. This was the secret discovered by Gandhi in dealing with the British rulers of India.

Now that I think about this notion, it seems very obvious. But it is the most obvious things in life that escape our notice—hence the welter of philosophic errors and confusion. Descartes described the genius as someone who never loses sight of first principles.

But the most important thing about this radical understanding of what self-awareness is, is the following. If I think of 'myself' primarily as a reality I am aware of when I reflect on myself, then 'myself' comes to mean a reality that I alone know about. I am my own private affair, my own private problem. I *infer* that you too 'have a self' just as I do, that you too turn in on yourself and wonder and worry. But I have no knowledge of yourself as you encounter yourself in your private reflection. As Eliot puts it in *The Waste Land*:

. . . I have heard the key
Turn in the door once and turn once only
We think of the key, each in his prison

Your reflection on yourself is your affair, as mine is my affair. And if self-awareness reduces to self-reflection, your self-awareness is your affair, as my self-awareness is my affair.

But if self-awareness precedes and is presupposed by self-reflection; if self-awareness is simply the vibrancy of myself; if self-awareness never stops; if self-awareness is simply my end of my address to you; *then* my self-awareness is something I am showing you, and your self-awareness is something you are showing me. That is why, when I appeal to someone for understanding, whether of a theological theory or of a painful personal problem, I am appealing to his or her self-awareness.

This continual exposure of our self-awareness goes back to our earliest childhood and is thus a long-established habit. So well established is it that we have ceased to notice it. And yet it is the basis of all human communication and thus is of inestimable importance and value for our self-understanding. From my earliest childhood, I acted out my feeling of myself, my self-awareness, encouraged by other people who were acting out theirs. I joked with my peers about the odd way Aunt Gladys acted out hers. And thus a *primary resonance* was set up between all the different self-awarenesses. Perhaps what happens when you experience a sharp dislike of someone or a deep misunderstanding is that between you the shared resonance started up as usual *and then* was jammed when the other person, or yourself, or both, turned in and got caught in some hang-up. This idea fits in exactly with a theory of guilt that I am working with—guilt as the felt friction between outgoingness and inturningness.

Self-awareness, then, is self-exposure: mine to you, yours to me. This is the primary mechanism of communication. I do not confront 'other bodies' but 'other selves'. And the existence of these other selves is not inferred from my own: it is known by a unique, a uniquely human interplay between dramatized self-awarenesses. In this interplay, we are not strangers to each other. We *become* strangers precisely through the above-named jamming of the interplay. If there were not the primary familiarity, community, resonance among people, people could not become strangers or enemies. And all the great religions strive to reactivate that primary level of interacting self-awareness. As we shall see, only a 'hearing' from God can fully reactivate it.

Here is another way of making the same point. I said at the beginning of this chapter that to limit self-awareness to reflective self-awareness is to say that 'myself' is absent from my normal awareness as is Iceland or the 'Titanic', and has to be recalled to consciousness just as they do. This makes me a stranger to myself, *and thus* makes all others strangers to me. Conversely, no longer a stranger to myself, no other is radically a stranger to me.

Now we must take a further step. The notion of self-awareness that we have been examining is not a *looking at* myself but a *being with* myself. That is the vital contrast. The notion we are excluding is the notion that I am only self-aware when I am turned in and looking at myself. In contrast with this notion, self-awareness is 'being with' myself. And this being-with myself, which I expose to others and which I recognize *in* others: this being-with myself that is my primary act of existing and that is my primary motive for living, my driving force, is a highly convinced and emotionally charged being-with. It is in fact self-love. The *life* of self-awareness is self-love. Self-awareness flowers as self-love. Self-love is as unavoidable as self-awareness. Self-love is self-awareness in life, in action, in interaction. Self-awareness without self-love is, in Eliot's phrase, 'a horror beyond your imagining' (*The Cocktail Party*). And so, just as self-awareness is self-exposure, so self-love is self-gift. The rareness with which self-love is realized in self-gift is due to the commonest incidence of the 'jamming factor', of a resonance that starts and then gets jammed. Of the 'jamming factor' there will be much to say, at the proper time.

To be for whom?: 1

The central desire grows out of the central condition of the human being, which is self-awareness/self-love. Appropriately it is the desire 'to be-for another'. I show that I love myself by the fact that I want this self that I love to be important to another. Experience testifies that there is no greater satisfaction than that of knowing that you count in the eyes of someone special, that that person's life is different because of you and happy because you're around.

It is wrongly supposed that people want to be important to each other because they don't feel important in themselves. On the contrary, it is because a person feels that he/she is 'special'—and it is impossible for the self-aware being *not* to feel 'special'—that he/she wants for this specialness to make a difference to another. The rage that neglect or contempt—especially by the beloved—causes in people is unaccountable for by any other hypothesis.

Now this desire to be-for is fated, it seems, to enjoy but partial satisfaction. When I love a person, I want to be-for that person. But must not that person remain to some extent a stranger to what it is *in me* that impels me to be-for her/him? Can *anyone* possibly know me the way I am aware of myself? And yet the *desire* to be-for that person springs direct from precisely this self-awareness/self-love.

Is the innate and constantly urging desire to be-for doomed to remain unsatisfied in its root-character deriving from my self-awareness? To say this would be to say that the desire is at root illusory: for what other name can we give to a desire for which there is no radical satisfaction? And to call this desire illusory would be to declare groundless the rage that people feel when they are not acknowledged. I do not feel rage at the frustration of a desire that is, in its ground, illusion, the illusion of being 'special'. Nor would I be able to describe this non-acknowledgement as *unjust*.

If we do *not* accept the 'illusion' hypothesis, but try to claim for human self-love the absolute status that, we obscurely feel, belongs to it, then we shall find ourselves drawing up a character-description of the 'other' for whom I *could* be beyond all disappointment and without 'meeting a stranger'—and it will be a character such as never existed!

Let us build up this character-sketch, and let us start with the radical question to which it would be the answer.

Who can I be-for as the person I am? Who can receive me, know me, as I feel myself? Such a being would have to have the following characteristics: (a) It would have to be experienced by me as totally inward to me, knowing me from within as no one else can; (b) It would have to be *without limit*, for it is another person's limitedness that makes him/her incapable of receiving me as I am; (c) It would have to be *other than myself*; (d) It would have to be other, however, not in the way that other persons are other, because this is due to their limitedness, and the being we are looking for has to be without limit. In what other way could this being be 'other'? Well, there is the 'otherness', to us, of the ultimate mystery in which all reality is felt to be somehow grounded. And if we went along this route and said, 'the being we're looking for is the ultimate mystery that grounds all there is', we would find that it fulfilled the *remaining three* requirements. For, being my very reason for existing, it would know me from within the way no one else can (a). And being the cause of all that is, it would be limitless, infinite (b). And of course it would be other, the other *for* which/whom I am (c).

At this point, Aquinas would say, 'and this is what all call God'. Note that we haven't proved that there is a God. What we have done is to point out that our inherent self-love makes us want 'to be-for', and that no other-person can penetrate to what it is in me that *wants* to 'be-for', so that the *desire* to be-for looks beyond other people to a mysterious all-understanding, all-accepting reality. What we have proved is not the existence *of God* but the existence of the *desire* for there to be God.

This desire for there to be God has been with the human race from the beginning: there has never, it seems, been humanity without religion, except for our era, what is loosely called 'modern times'. The most significant and influential denial of the validity of religion was Feuerbach's *The Essence of Christianity* early in the last century. Feuerbach had a devastating effect, for he was really the first writer to say that religion was wishful thinking, that man 'wishes into being' a God who will be just, merciful, loving, understanding—all qualities that man feels *in himself* but somehow never realizes or enjoys. We dream up a God who responds to these desires of the human soul. Marx was enthralled with that book. As far as he was concerned, Feuerbach had dealt the death-blow to religion. And most intellectuals thought the same.

No one realized at the time that to say that belief in God is wishful thinking is not to say there is no God. It is not to say anything, either way, about the existence or non-existence of God. Such a conclusion is a huge logical slip. Of course belief in God is wishful thinking. So is falling in love. So is engaging in any great creative adventure. On the contrary, if there were *no* wish for God to exist, that would create serious—I would say insuperable—problems for religion.

What I have done in this chapter is to spell out, in terms of my idea of the basic human desire, the wishful thinking that God exists. I've 'done a Feuerbach', not with sublime ideas like justice, mercy, love, understanding, but with the core-idea of self-love and the desire it generates 'to be-for'.

Now one may perhaps conclude, from the fact that our central desire is not totally fulfillable through human relationships but only in commitment to God, that we should seek fulfilment in this commitment rather than in human relationships. No conclusion could be more erroneous. On the contrary, the effect of experiencing the more radical fulfilment of our desire to be-for (in God) is that one will experience that desire more intensely in relation to other persons. For, experiencing myself as 'special' absolutely and 'for God', for the ultimate mystery, I have a much fuller conviction of my specialness *as* a gift to others. Thus in the gospel the presence and experiencing of God creates a new depth in human community, called by Jesus 'the Kingdom of God', the polity of God, the politics of God. No God-experience that bypasses the community can be a valid God-experience. Jesus sums this principle up when he says that the first and greatest commandment is 'to love the Lord thy God with all thy strength' and that the second, 'to love thy neighbour as thyself', *is like the first*. It is the first in social terms. One cannot love another without loving oneself. It follows that *until* a person has that fullness of self-love which is only found in being-for God, he or she is correspondingly restricted in the power to love the neighbour.

To be for whom?: 2

The very thing in us that makes us want to be for another is destined to be forever unknown *by* the other. This is the heart of the human problem—an ineluctable inner loneliness that, spelt out, is a desire that there be, in fact, the only possible partner to it: one as intimate to me as I am, unlimited by him/herself, really other but with the otherness of the ultimate all-grounding mystery: the desired partner to our ultimate loneliness.

How is this desire experienced by people? I think we can discern three states of the desire. First, as it is in everybody, largely unrecognized, perhaps not recognized at all. People in this condition would experience the inner loneliness *only indirectly*, in the restlessness and discontent of life. They would not advert to it or name it to themselves *as* a condition of loneliness. Second, there are the people who *awake* to the inner loneliness, who experience it, suffer it, but who do not yet experience it *as* the desire for the mysterious partner. They experience it, simply, as an inner longing that can never be satisfied. The best way to understand this middle condition is to point out that *another* person, intimate to the person who is in it—a spouse, say, or a close friend—would be able to see, in the person's behaviour, a seemingly hopeless pursuit of a partner such as could never exist, a partner who somehow *is* the person yet is other, loving and sustaining. And if the spouse or friend was in state 3—shortly to be described—he/she would probably say, 'Of course, it's really God they want.' For the person in state 3 has made the leap of faith. This leap is not an irrational leap in the dark. In one sense, it is very rational, for it consists in believing that a desire that is central to my being and living, and that no human other can satisfy, *is not in vain*, does not come from nowhere: and that is rational—to say that our deep and inescapable feelings *are not without reason*. On the other hand, it is an act of enormous trust to believe that there *is* the other that satisfies the desire, for

14

this other is not anything in our familiar world. Faith means trusting our radical desire even when it reaches beyond our familiar world, finding nothing there to satisfy it. It is a combination of the rational—believing that the radical desire that governs all human living is not ultimately without a reason for being—and the beyond-rational—saying 'Yes' to an unknown, mysterious, mysteriously desired 'other'.

The middle state is of enormous importance. James Baldwin, the most important black writer of the sixties, wrote a novel about five years ago, *Just Above My Head*. The novel begins with, and concludes with, the suicide of a young black gospel singer who is the principal character. Arthur has charisma. He can draw into his visionary singing a vast audience. His songs are songs of an eternal loneliness with Jesus as the only healer. But Arthur is not a believer. He is thoroughly disillusioned with Church in all forms. Through these songs, and through the enormous psychic force that comes into him from the crowd, he experiences himself as eternally lonely and desirous of the impossible. This makes him very vulnerable—in addition to which he is homosexual. He is emotionally exploited by all sorts of people, some very much degraded. Arthur, I believe, is a powerful example of state 2.

State 2 is probably very common; in a sense we're all in it! A wise priest once said to me, 'Alcoholism is a thirst for God', and I could make little sense of this comment at the time. But we begin to get a dramatically different picture of the human world when we consider that human desperation may come 'from above' as well as 'from below', that anxiety and depression may not be fully accountable for as a being pulled *down* from normal healthy social life, but may be an experience of emptiness that looks *above* the human condition for its remedy. And clinical psychology *is* beginning to look in this direction. There is emerging a 'fourth force', calling itself transpersonal psychology. ('First force' is behaviourism; 'second force' is Freud et al.; 'Third Force' is Abraham Maslow's self-actualization.)

The case of alcoholism is especially instructive. For Alcoholics Anonymous seek to bring the client to a point of absolute belief in the power of God alone to lift him/her out of the enslavement. It lays this directive down, *not* because of any religious affiliation—Protestant, Catholic, etc.—for it has none, but simply *because nothing else works*. I would suggest, as a theological interpretation of their success, that this is because the *desire* that can make people desperate

15

and lead to alcoholism and other drugs is the desire for the mysterious partner.

Nietzsche bears a witness to our God-desire so powerful that it is terrifying. His description of the Madman in *The Gay Science* is one of the most important theological texts in the last five centuries. Nietzsche was atheistic, nihilistic and, for the last ten years of his life, in an insane asylum. But what *drove* him mad was that he *saw* the depth of the human need for God, and consequently what emptiness we were condemning ourselves to in leaving worship out of our culture—an emptiness that only a new race, of 'supermen', would be courageous enough to sustain. That description of the Madman with the lantern crying out, 'How have we been able to drink up the sea?', is a classic description of state 2:

The Madman. Have you not heard of that madman who lit a lantern in the bright morning hours, ran to the market place, and cried incessantly, 'I seek God! I seek God!' As many of those who did not believe in God were standing around just then, he provoked much laughter. Why, did he get lost? said one. Did he lose his way like a child? said another. Or is he hiding? Is he afraid of us? Has he gone on a voyage? or emigrated? Thus they yelled and laughed. The madman jumped into their midst and pierced them with his glances.

'Whither is God' he cried. 'I shall tell you. *We have killed him—* you and I. All of us are his murderers. But how have we done this? How are we able to drink up the sea? Who gave us the sponge to wipe away the entire horizon? What did we do when we unchained this earth from its sun? Whither is it moving now? Whither are we moving now? Away from all suns? Are we not plunging continually? Backward, sideward, forward, in all directions? Is there any up or down left? Are we not straying as through an infinite nothing? Do we not feel the breath of empty space? Has it not become colder? Is not night and more night coming on all the while? Must not lanterns be lit in the morning? Do we not hear anything yet of the noise of the gravediggers who are burying God? Do we not smell anything yet of God's decomposition? Gods too decompose. God is dead. God remains dead. And we have killed him. How shall we, the murderers of all murderers, comfort ourselves? What was holiest and most powerful of all that the world has yet owned has bled to death under our knives. Who will wipe this blood off us? What water is there for us to clean ourselves? What festivals of atonement, what sacred games shall we have to invent? Is not the greatness of this deed too great for us? Must not we ourselves become gods simply to seem worthy of it? There has never been a greater deed; and whoever will be born after us—for the sake of this deed he will be part of a higher history than all history hitherto.'

Here the madman fell silent and looked again at his listeners; and they too were silent and stared at him in astonishment. At last they threw his lantern to the ground, and it broke and went out. 'I come too early', he said then; 'my time has not come yet. This tremendous event is still on its way, still wandering—it has not yet reached the ears of man. Lightning and thunder require time, the light of the stars requires time, deeds require time even after they are done, before they can be seen and heard. This deed is still more distant from them than the most distant stars—*and yet they have done it themselves.*'

It has been related further than on that same day the madman entered divers churches and there sang his *requiem aerternam deo.* Led out and called to account, he is said to have replied each time, 'What are these churches now if they are not the tombs and sepulchres of God?' (*The Gay Science*, section 125).

17

The other within changes the other without

Implicit in the last two chapters is a definition of God. God is the other within that ends an otherwise ineluctable inner loneliness. Or: God is the ground of being within each person that ends an otherwise ineluctable inner loneliness.

Of course God cannot be defined. God is the one reality that cannot be defined. All that a definition can do here is to say *why* God cannot be defined: and this *can* be with varying degrees of accuracy. The 'partner' to the otherwise ineluctable inner loneliness of the person *is* unimaginable, incomprehensible, unlimited, indefinable: but in saying that this infinitely mysterious reality partners our inner aloneness and that nothing else can, we are saying a great deal.

As I have already indicated, this opening to 'the other within' does not give a person a private hideout. The reason lies in the *nature* of this 'other'. For this other, being *my* reason for being, is *everybody's* reason for being; being *my* ground, is *everybody's* ground; being *my* transcendent inner self, is *everybody's* transcendent inner self. To feel a touch of God is to be in sympathy with those 'millions of points of view' of which Anna speaks in *Mr God, This is Anna*. (Actually she coined her own word for impossibly big numbers: 'squillions'.)

Descending from these lofty heights of speculation to more immediate experience, we can describe the practical effect, on human intercourse, of being awakened to 'the other within'. 1. We have seen that it is the sense of myself as special that motivates my going out to others and seeks positive relationships. Now if I am opened to 'the other within', I know my worth not only from myself but from the ground of all being, and this means that I am far more convinced of my worth, my significance in the world, and so am much more motivated to move out to others. The exemplar of this condition is Jesus who, *because* he deeply knows himself to be special

18

in God's sight, embraces in love the whole world. Thus the pre-Jesus command 'to love your neighbour as yourself' takes on a new intensity when, knowing yourself loved by God, you love yourself far more than you otherwise can and thus love your neighbour far more. John's Gospel expresses this fuller self-love and its community dimension, in Jesus' command, 'Love one another *as I have loved you.*'

2. People who are being liberated from the ineluctable inner loneliness of the human are freer for each other. The reason is that the radical unknowability of persons to each other is no longer a source of mistrust. If it is only the intimacy between two persons that is the alternative to their radical strangeness to each other, then there is going to be some fear that this strangeness will threaten the intimacy. But intraself friendship is *another* alternative to this strangeness, taking the pressure off intimacy, releasing intimacy from bearing the whole burden, and thus of course making intimacy itself much freer. To put all this in simpler, evangelical language, children of God are not a threat to one another. To go into a very different idiom, lovers of God should have better sexual relationships.

3. The third consequence is really the converse of the second. If intimacy is not my only protection from feeling threatened by the other, then I can reach out in love to others with whom I am not and cannot be intimate. Thus there flows out of the openness to 'the other within' that capacity for universal love that is a primary feature of all the world religions.

Narcissism and God

We have found that human desire, reduced to its nucleus, opens up the question of God. This desire turns out to be the desire to be-for another, and this raises the question of God *in two ways*. I want to look again at these two approaches, then to suggest that they reduce to one approach, and then to bring out some of the implications of this single approach.

1. The first approach has for its starting-point a startlingly strange fact, a seeming paradox. It consists in noting that the thing that drives me to seek to be important and enhancing in another's life is a conviction that I am unique, special and precious. It is a nucleic self-love that impels me to form relationships. Now the startling thing is that this very sense of myself that thus directs me towards the other is destined to be forever unknown, unentered, *by* the other. No one can feel me as I feel myself. To do so, the other would have to *be* me. So it seems that the very thing in me that impels me to come into community is itself doomed to an eternal loneliness. Unless there is some quite other kind of partner.

Next, I assemble a kind of identikit for this strange partner. There seem to be four features: (a) it must be as intimate to me as I am to myself; (b) it must be without limit, without that *kind* of self which would forbid its total entry into *my* self; (c) but it must be other, for this seemingly eternal inner loneliness is precisely a craving for relationships; (d) but it must not be other in the way other people are other, for this is the way of limit, excluded by (b).

What might this 'other otherness' be? I suggest, as answer, 'the otherness of the ultimate mystery that is the condition of our existence and of existence itself'. This is 'what all call God'. And then I check out this result, arriving at (d), with (a) (b) and (c). At (a), I recall that the mystical tradition unanimously describes God as 'closer to me than I am to myself'. At (b), God is of his/her/its nature without limit, and at (c) God, we realize, surely *is* other than

20

what he/she/it creates and sustains in being. Thus we arrive at a definition of God as 'the other within, that ends an otherwise ineluctable inner loneliness'.

2. Taking this same fact, that my well-being is a 'being for', I now explore not the *fulfilment* of a being that works this way, but the *ground*, or origin, or cause of such a being. This spontaneous other-enhancement, this hedonic relationality, is neither reducible to our animal beginnings nor accountable for as *our* creation, as of our making, as are our decisions. We do not make love any more than we make 'the light of setting suns'. Thus we need to look beyond ourselves for the source and purpose of our hedonic-altruistic existence.

And just as, in (1), we 'borrowed' at the crucial point from the universally attested sense of mystery, so here we 'borrow', at the crucial point, from an ancient philosophic tradition. When we wonder *how*, in what direction, to 'go beyond ourselves', we recall an idea in that tradition: that what the human being *has*, that God *is*; that what, in the creature, are *qualities* are, in the Creator, *essence*. The *way* in which this philosophy saw our qualities as *coming-from* God was to regard God *as* those qualities, in essence, an infinite essence in which we are, as it were, dipped and thus endowed with those qualities. The simplistic platonic notion that the *idea* of tree was a perfection beyond 'trees', in which all trees participated and so got their 'tree-ness', was transposed to give an idea of a transcendent creative super-essence whence all beings have their qualities.

But what is *meant* by God's 'being' what we 'have'? Do we not find that, as we cross the gulf between qualities as we know them— of generosity, of intelligence, of humour and so on—and this mysterious reality that *is* those qualities, our thought comes apart, there is nothing for it to hold onto?

But then we notice a rather exciting thing. In the particular human quality that we have been exploring throughout, namely, the quality of 'flourishing *in* being-for', we can get an inkling of the divine identity of 'being' with 'quality' *on our side of the gulf*. For it is the most important and satisfying human experience that, in the consciousness of being for another, in the consciousness of this *quality* of other-enhancement with myself, I experience in quite a new way that 'I am'. This new density of selfhood in the lover is the central theme of love-poetry. Thus I *can* know *my* being as being-for, as love, and so look beyond *this* experience to a grounding

21

reality that simply and absolutely *is* in being for all, that simply and absolutely 'enjoys itself' *in* nurturing all. This reality remains a mystery for me, as it is when I try equating it with 'intelligence' and other qualities, but in this case I have a springboard. I *am* a springboard. I sense a mystery *in myself* that impels me towards this origin.

Now let us look at these two approaches together. The first approach seeks out God as the *desired*, as the desiderated partner to free us from the otherwise ineluctable loneliness. The scholastics would say that we are here speaking of God as 'final cause'. The second approach seeks out God as the *origin*, as that which needs to be posited to *ground* our hedonic relationality. The scholastics would call this the pursuit of God as 'efficient cause'. The first approach pivots about an otherwise ineluctable loneliness, the second pivots about an otherwise unaccountable excellence.

Perhaps the most important thing to notice, however, in comparing the two approaches, is this. The first approach is *much more concrete and experiential*. It speaks of loneliness—the loneliness that creates alcoholism and the many other forms of human desperation—and seeks a partner. But it has to take a rather roundabout way to establish that this 'partner' is indeed God the creator of all that is—the device of the 'identikit'. The second approach, however, is more abstract. It starts with an abstract question: 'Where does our hedonic-relationality come from?' But it gets to God much more directly, through the identifying of 'quality' with 'being'.

In sum: in the first approach, the self and its dire need is very evident, and God as the unique satisfier less so. In the second approach, God is more centre-stage, but the self is considered more theoretically.

Must there not be an approach that combines these two, in which they meet and correct each other's imbalance? In which 'God' would be clearly God-the-all-creating *and* the self's most deeply desired partner? In which I would be, *at once*, wording 'what everyone wants' *and* speaking of 'what everyone calls God'?

I think that there is. In the depths of my ultimate loneliness, where none can reach me, I want there to be Another whose very 'to be' is 'to be for me', whose selfhood is not a selfhood into which he must ultimately retreat leaving me in mine. Quite frankly, I want a partner with whom I can have it both ways: constitutionally involved with me, and constitutionally other than me. And this *is* 'what all call God'.

The thing to notice here is that God's nature as an identity of 'being himself' and 'being-for' is coming in as the *immediately and desperately desired partner to my loneliness*, and not simply as a beautiful theoretical construct, as in the second approach. *I* have just *got to have* God that way—as I've just got to have food and sex—only more deeply so, more achingly so.

It will certainly be objected that this is an amazingly self-centred approach. I would prefer to call it an honest one. The objection arises, I believe, from the long-built-up habit of inattention to the inner loneliness deemed by our culture non-remediable and therefore treated as non-existent, its recrudescence as sickness (I remember Eliot's fine description of Blake, in *Selected Essays*, as seeing into 'the essential strength and sickness of the human soul'). God is indeed the deepest and most unavowed dream of our narcissism. What could be more narcissistic than the saying of Angelus Silesius, 'If God stopped thinking about me, he would cease to exist'? The saying is strictly orthodox. A God, who *is* being, who could forget *a* being, would be a blasphemous obscenity. God *is* 'a thinking about me and about all that is'.

The trick is that once this God has caught us by our narcissism and we are in love with him/her, then we learn that our lover has interests everywhere and that these interests must be ours. The first stage, of 'getting caught by our narcissism', is the 'first age' of the spiritual life. It leads out into what Eliot calls 'the dark cold and the empty desolation', the 'Dark Night of the Soul', the second age ('East Coker' from *Four Quartets*). Through the darkness we come into the 'spiritual marriage', the third and final age. The mystical tradition is astonishingly unanimous about this structure. We shall see it perfectly realized in the experience of the disciples of Jesus.

Thus in the very heart and core of human loneliness is inscribed the divinity of its only possible partner. My inner loneliness is the desire for another who *is* thought for me. One who *is* thought is 'what all call God'. Rather than accept such a companion, Nietzsche declared the world meaningless. Such is the human soul.

God the hedonist: 1

The most important fact about the human condition is that, at root, self-love and self-gift are one, that self-love flowers in self-giving, flowers *as* self-giving. This radical oneness between the way pleasure works and the way self-gift works makes it to be the case that pleasure finds its full intensity only in self-gift, and self-gift loses every last trace of moralism and condescension in pleasure.

This radical oneness of self-love with self-gift is not of our making. Of this we have reason to be glad, for it means that it is safe from our power to destroy—and if we are not deeply persuaded of that power, we are still innocent of history.

Perhaps because it is not of our making, we do not easily believe in it. We *experience* it, in loving, but we do not easily accord to this experience the recognition of believing. This means that we are in the strange position of enjoying this deep beauty of ourselves without believing in it. We snatch at it, as it were, as though it were too good to be true and we were stealing something that did not belong to us.

The reason for this attitude is a deep distrust of happiness, of free, unconditional joy, in the human mind. There is a certain natural pessimism, parsimony, puritanism about the way we think of ourselves. Thus we keep the core-experience, of enjoying ourselves in making another happy, in a kind of limbo of the too-good-to-be-true.

As I suggested in the paragraph before last, our real 'interest' in keeping the unity of self-love with self-gift unacknowledged is that we can thus avoid acknowledging as central to our life something that is not of our making. A thin, cramped view of human existence is the price we pay for regarding it as something wholly within our control. We can discern this note of self-inflicted poverty, of a kind of dutiful grimness, in much so-called humanist thinking. We prefer making life difficult to being grateful to it. For if it is difficult, that is the surest and most reassuring sign that it is of our making. We easily take credit for hard work.

The extreme opposite of this natural puritanism is belief in God. We have not begun to realize how outrageous belief in God *is* to our exiguous, self-originated philosophy of the human. For that belief not only brings back out of its limbo the core-experience of finding our intensest pleasure in other-enhancement: it goes outrageously further and says that this core-experience is a participation in a reality for whom 'to be' *is* 'to love', for whom 'to be' *is* 'to be for'. As Meister Eckhart, the fourteenth-century Dominican mystic, beautifully puts it: God enjoys himself and wants us to join him.

Let me spell this idea out a bit. For the human being, 'to be *well*' is 'to be-for', but simply 'to *be*' is not the same as 'to be-for'. God *is* this perfection which we *have* by participating in his being. For the human being, 'to be well' is 'to be for' because the human derives from, depends upon, is originated and shaped by an ultimate reality whose very being, whose being *at all*, is being-for. And *because* this reality is the ultimately and all-embracingly real, there *is* no 'other' for it the meeting of whose claims would not be identical with its own happiness. The ground of the human condition, of flourishing in making-flourish, is a 'being', or a 'beyond-being', in whom the very *distinction* between flourishing and making-flourish does not exist.

If there is God, then the hedonism that hides, in all of us, from the stern demands of our self-made life is unconditionally legitimated. It is not legitimated *against* the demands of duty, rather it embraces and fulfills those demands in the 'grace' of him/her who knows nothing of pleasure-against-duty.

It looks as though we have stumbled on something rather like Kant's proof for the existence of God. Kant, incidentally, did a good thing with the old idea of proving that God is. He said we couldn't do it, but that what we could do was to show that the most important and precious things in our life make a great deal more sense if there *is* God. Belief in God gives ample breathing-space to these precious things. We pass from arguments that are 'necessary but unsatisfying' to a style of argument that is 'not necessary but satisfying'. The 'precious thing' I have been talking about is the radical one-ness of self-love with self-gift. And Kant's 'moral argument' was that God was the condition for an ultimate reconciliation, in us, of the demand for happiness with the demand of duty.

To sum up. The unity of self-love with self-gift is not in our hands, and for this reason we do not easily recognize it. The full recognition of it is belief in an all-constituting reality that is a happiness that is in love. To love himself is to love all that is. To enjoy himself is to pour out joy on all that is.

God the hedonist: 2

Our biggest obstacle to believing in God is our innate distrust of happiness. This is a disbelief in our goodness. We do not easily believe that, through no work or merit of ours, our deepest desire is to make another person happy. We do not believe in this spontaneous goodness of ourselves.

I have long wondered whether it is the fact that happiness is not of our making that causes us to distrust it, or whether it is something closer to happiness itself that causes this distrust. Once you spell it out like that, it is surely the latter. One of our most deeply operative scripts is 'too good to be true!' Greek tragedy—the original tragedy—is all about 'hubris', which might be called 'happiness going to a person's head and inviting the vengeance of the gods'.

Perhaps the best solution of the above dilemma is to say that we have two sides of the same thing: one side is distrust of what is not in our control; the other is preference for what *is* in our control. One is fear of the unknown; the other is preference for the known. But doesn't this make it still clearer which is the controlling side, which causes which? It is the dynamite of desire for boundless bliss that we are afraid of, and this fear drives us into the arms of a smaller, self-made, self-marked, familiar world.

The first step, then, is to learn to trust this desire. It, and not what we make of ourselves, is who we are. At root, we are happy sources of happiness in each other.

Let us take this notion a step further. Perhaps the principal way we justify the distrust of happiness is that we tell ourselves that happiness is a selfish thing. We must not live for ourselves, we say, but for others. So under the guise of morality, we tell the big lie about ourselves, which is the denial of the goodness, the rightness, of the desire for boundless bliss.

Notice that I've slipped something more into the discussion. To 'the denial of desire' I have added 'denial of the goodness, of the

27

rightness, of desire'. Denial of desire means denying (to ourselves) that we *have* the desire, and this is surely different from denying the *goodness* of desire. But is it really? Isn't there at least a causal connection between the two denials? The basic 'too-good-to-be-true' script triggers another, namely 'happiness is selfish, and selfish is wrong'.

Thus it is necessary to recognize not only that we *have* the desire for limitless happiness, but that this is 'as it should be', this is 'right', this is who and what and why we are, this is what life is all about. We have to reverse the basic tape so thoroughly that this causes reversal of the other, 'moral' tape.

Now once we begin to get comfortable with this way of thinking, outlandish as it is for our culture, we begin to see the world in a new way, and very strange it all begins to look. For what kind of a world is it, in which the pursuit of happiness is the pursuit of reality? What kind of a world is it, such that our best clue to its nature and meaning is the sense we have that we are meant to be happy, that happiness is right and good and therefore conformed to the real nature of things?

Then we begin to be ready to contemplate the most extraordinary possibility conceivable: that the *reason* why happiness is good and 'right' and in touch with reality is that reality is grounded in, and wholly shaped by, happiness: that the source of being is a beyond-being that enjoys itself without limit *and therefore* not at the cost of but to the advantage of all that exists. That identity, in us, of 'being *well*' with 'being-for', in which we find it so hard to believe, derives from an identity of 'being *at all*' with 'being for all'. We just begin to be able to think of God as a limitless act of enjoyment which, by being happy, creates and nurtures and fosters and promotes. God enjoys himself and tries to woo us into joining him, overcoming our resistance to happiness which ultimately is resistance to him/her. Here is a saying of Charles de Foucauld: 'My beloved is happy, and this fills me with a profound happiness that I have to spread.' For this reason the 'Little Brothers and Sisters' follow in his footsteps, contemplatives who seek God in the desert and among the poor and destitute.

We say that God is love, but this assertion is often hollow. It is hollowed by our disbelief in happiness, for our distrust of happiness begets an idea of 'unselfishness', of a 'love' that has nothing to do with that deep dark desire within us that is 'purely altruistic': and then we extend this idea to infinity and think that is what God is like. We project onto God our failure to be honest with ourselves. And this infinite do-gooder does us no good at all!

With a hand I did not know was mine I clasp the unknown hand of my happiness leading me out of the solemn prison of myself.

God the hedonist: 3

First let me recapitulate, rather more clearly, the main line of argument. The human being, as intelligent, is the image of the one who *is* intelligence and thus is the source of all intelligence. But I have no idea what it would be to be my intelligence, so I do not know what the mirror mirrors. The human being, as spontaneous lover, is the image of the one who *is* love, and I do have an inkling of what it would be to be the love of someone: for when I love, I sense, with an altogether new intensity, that *I am*. To love is to feel in oneself the current that flows out of the heart of all existence.

Now we must take a further step. My happiness is mine and not yours. Your happiness is yours and not mine. In a good relationship, my happiness advances yours, and yours mine. That is the meaning of a good relationship. But my happiness remains mine and not yours, and yours remains yours and not mine.

My happiness can always increase, so there is no limit to how happy I can be. I am open to infinite happiness. But even were I infinitely happy, this infinite happiness would still be 'of me' and not of someone else. It follows that the limit on happiness is 'on the side of the *subject*' and not in the *amount* of happiness. Its only limit is 'in being mine and not someone else's'.

Now in the happiness that is God, there is no such limit. Of this, it may not be said that it is God's and not someone else's. For God is not a subject who *has* happiness: he/she *is* happiness—just as he/she *is* being, *is* intelligence, *is* love. So God's happiness *is* the happiness of all things: it is not his as opposed to theirs. In being his/hers, in being God, it *is* theirs, ours.

Now the happiness that is God, where it exists in a being that is not happy, is compassion. It is precisely because the happiness of God is in every being as its happiness that God can have (and be) compassion for that being when the being is not happy. If you like,

God's compassion is God's happiness in a being wanting to be experienced by the being but being blocked, for whatever reason.

The truth, the nature and the meaning of the divine compassion is the most important theological problem of our time. For our century has seen more human slaughter than any other. The number of those violently slaughtered has been estimated at two hundred million in Gil Elliot's book *The Twentieth Century Book of the Dead*: he can only afford six pages for the Holocaust. Apart from slaughter, most people on this planet are gnawed by unremitting hunger, and all over the world the torture of humanity is compounded by the tyrannies of communist ideology and capitalist greed. It is a terrible picture. And no serious believer in God can escape the question 'Does God care?' If he does care, why doesn't he stop the torture, and if he can't, how can he be God?

I don't think the problem lies here. If God were forcibly to prevent people from inflicting cruelty, he would be curtailing their freedom, and *then* he would not be God. No, the real problem is: how may we *think* of God as caring, as solidary with the weak, the poor, the oppressed, the tortured? More precisely, how is his infinity, his eternity, his immortality, able to identify itself with the suffering of this world?

Medieval theology never solved this problem. To it, infinity and immortality remained beyond the grasp of pain. Perfection excluded the imperfection of suffering.

Modern theology has reacted strongly against this position and insisted on the compassionate nature of God—with the Bible, incidentally, for the Bible, being imaginative and poetic rather than philosophical, does not have this problem.

But modern theology tends to fall into the trap of *so* identifying God with human suffering as to *limit* God. It tends to think up a God who, like us, is bewildered and suffering. This is understandable, for *can* there be compassion except on the part of one who *in himself, in herself*, knows weakness and limitation? Surely compassion is *of* the limited.

I want to suggest that this is not true: that on the contrary there is a mysterious divine compassion that consists precisely in its possessor's happiness *in all beings* and not just *in himself*; that consists precisely *in* the infinity, the eternity, the perfection of God. It is the freedom of God's happiness from being 'his and not mine' that makes it to be compassion in those who suffer.

For the essence of compassion is that the compassionate person

31

is in, and with, the sufferer. But no being is able to be in, and with, me as closely as is God, whose being *is* my being, whose happiness *is* my happiness. 'The other within who ends an otherwise ineluctable inner loneliness' is a happiness in which I have my being; and the meaning of religious conversion is that I come to experience this happiness. It is *the happiness* of God that is intimate to the sufferer. It is *as happy* that God is intimate to the sufferer.

The supreme example we have of the compassionate presence of God's happiness to the human being oppressed by all the evil of this world is the crucifixion of Jesus. The resurrection is God's eternal happiness 'coming through' and showing *all* human suffering as concealing the healing joy of God. In the resurrection encounters of the disciples, the compassion of God becomes *known*, in its blissful centre and in its presence to the suffering.

In short, compassion is an infinite happiness trying to realize itself in a tortured world. 'God enjoys himself and wants us to join him.'

Note: It has been suggested that this insight into the happiness of God in all creation is profoundly Jewish and permeates the Jewish Scriptures that Christian tradition has got into the habit of calling 'The Old Testament'—a habit we should now be considering breaking. It has also been suggested that the psychological root of Christian anti-Semitism, one of the worst blemishes of Christian history, is Christians' discomfort with their natural goodness and with the way it opens to God. They repress it, in the interest of making their own goodness, and they see the repressed part of themselves symbolized in the Jew. Similarly, white racism may be based on an unavowed hatred, by the whites, of their own spontaneity, symbolized by the black.

Defining God by human need: 1

When I succeed in giving expression to my inner loneliness—that is, to *why* I am lonely, to *what* I am lonely without, this is what I come up with: I want, as my companion, an 'I am' who, of his/her nature, arouses the 'I am' of me. This is the definition of God *by* the inner loneliness of the human being, a most urgent need of our time. The crucial phase is 'of his/her nature'. Take that out, and you have the description of a good relationship between two human beings. Each of us is an 'I am', and in a creative relationship my 'I am' arouses your 'I am'. But your 'I am' brings out my 'I am' through a quality, a vitality, a vibrancy that goes *through* you: your 'I am' does not *of its nature* awaken mine, is not of its nature the awakening of mine. This becomes plain when we consider that, in being someone for another, you feel *more* of a someone. Now this selfhood in you, that *increases* when you relate creatively to another, existed before you met that other, was already there *to* increase with meeting. So the self that undoubtedly lives more fully to another had already a life apart from that other. With the 'inner companion' this is not so. God has no 'self' apart from me, no self 'before he met me', no self into which he retreats leaving me in myself. God 'of his nature' companions me, is for me. God *is*—by nature, by definition—'thinking-about-me', 'thinking-about-you', 'thinking-about-the-world'. God is—by nature, by definition—'being-for-me', 'being-for-you', 'being-for-the-world'. The statement of Angelus Silesius, 'If God stopped thinking of me he would cease to exist', is strictly orthodox: God, by definition, *is* 'thinking-of-me'.

And each of us *wants* him to be that way. Our inner loneliness wills there to be the one who *is* for me, whose 'is' is for me, whose 'am' is for me, whose being is for me, whose 'to be' is for me. Our inner loneliness is *at once* an infinite narcissism (I want to be totally understood) and an infinite love-requirement (I want my companion to be other, challenging, demanding). In our inner loneliness we want it both ways. God, by definition, lets us *have* it both ways, combines the absolutely intimate with the absolutely other.

One eloquent sign of the truth of this assertion is that people are constantly making the demand for this kind of combination of intimate-with-other *on each other*. People demand of their spouses that they be God for them, and of course they can't. People try to fulfill *with each other* the insatiable requirement of the inner loneliness, to be totally entered and led forth into the whole ecstasy of existence. That there *is* this need for God in us is shown by the fact that we demand of each other to *be* God for us.

There would be a wonderful renovation of human life if people could discover how their inner need *is* satisfied—by the One who *of his nature* satisfies it—and so cease to make the impossible demand on each other, leave each other free to be finite, to *have* concerns and troubles of their own. But it's more than *ceasing* to make the God-demand on each other. It is allowing the divine being-for to work through us, relating us to each other. For that 'being-for' that we do not have 'by nature' we do have *by participation* in the One who does, the One who *is* it by nature. In *Conversations Between Buddha and Jesus* by Carrin Dunne we read:

> *Jesus*: You are right in saying that the only reality is Being. It alone is serious and all the rest is jest. Yes, the young physician will be truly happy if what he loves is Being. His happiness no one can take away. But consider this: suppose it happened that Being itself should fall in love with beings. Suppose Being took beings seriously. What would happen then?

> *Gotama*: You speak of Being as though it were a person, an individuality.

> *Jesus*: The only one, strictly speaking. Who alone is not trapped in selfishness and cut off from reality by concern over his own individuality, since that individuality is Being itself. Being is my Father's secret name.

Note that the idea of human love as *participating* in the love that God is incorporates the second way—God as source—in the first—God as end, as desired. We now have the one way.

Defining God by human need: 2

What the definition does is to take the basic dynamic of *human* relations, which is the dynamic of 'being well in being-for' and totally to transform it by the phrase 'of his/her nature'. The inner companion, the inner other, is 'for me' of his/her nature. This means 'by definition': take away the 'for-me' from God, and you take away everything. God *is* 'being-for'. That is his/her 'nature'. Why do I say that? How do I know? Well, try saying it's the whole *idea* of God, it's what people are trying to find words for when they try to talk of God. Talking about God is trying to take away limit and still make sense. This means taking some quality we value—such as love or intelligence—and saying that God does not *have* this quality, so that his 'character' would limit its operation, he *is* it (and this, note, means 'he originates it, he is why there *is* love, intelligence, etc.'). And since the quality we are here considering is 'being-for', we say that God is *by nature, by definition*, being-for. His being-for is not self-restricted, as our being-for another is restricted by the self. And I, in my insatiable inner loneliness and terror, *want* a companion who is *unrestrictedly* 'for me', un-self-restrictedly for me.

I think this description of God is important, for the following reason. In this enormously introspective and experience-centred age, we need a description of God *in terms of human need* that coincides with *what has always been understood* to be the meaning of 'God'. The idea of God we are looking for must be *at once* 'what humans most deeply *want*' *and* connote transcendence, beyondness, that is, what humans have always *known* to be what God is. That is the theological enterprise: the learning to *recognize*, in the texture of human experience as we express it in science, art, drama, therapy and so on, a desire for what is traditionally expressed as mysterious, transcendent, infinite and so on. Until people make this connection, their belief is liable to be an escape *from* the human problem *into* 'the beyond'.

35

My definition makes the connection. The *link*, in it, between the contemporary and the timeless, between the human ache and the eternal idea, is in the phrase 'of his nature'. I, hungry, insatiable, lonely being, *want* 'one who loves me un-self-restrictedly', one who 'of his nature', *is* 'love for me'. And thousands of years of philosophical thinking agree that God—if God there be—*is*, by nature, un-self-restricted love, un-self-restricted intelligence. The human heart, up against itself now in all its bafflement and despair, says *the same thing* about its desired liberator that the philosophical tradition has always said about 'God': that he/she is un-self-restricted out-goingness: that God's self-enjoyment *is* outgoingness, *is* being for all.

As Jesus says to Buddha, in Carrin Dunne's fantasy, God is 'being in person'. This means '*being* as love, *being* as us-directed, *being* as me-directed'. And this means a me-directedness which, being what God *is*, cannot turn itself off. And this is what I, in my loneliness and terror, want. I want 'being in my favour'. I want 'reality in my favour'. Never mind that this is egoism. It is *us*, whether we like it or not.

A simpler way of putting this may be to say that one who was my lover *in the nature of things*, as no human lover can be, would have to be the source of 'the nature of things': 'what all call God'. And that's what we're after in this whole theological enterprise: a description of God out of our experienced inner need that is describing 'what all call God'.

It may help at this stage if we recall the 'two ways' before they came together. We saw that in the first way (desire) our need/desire is clearly ours, God less clearly God. In the second way, it's the other way round. The human end is less urgent—curiosity about our origin—but God is more clearly God. This is because 'God as origin, as source of the nature of things' is more clearly God than is 'God as the desired of human beings'. The advantage of the approach I am taking is that the more obscure (but much more vital to us) God of desire is seen at last to have the clearer features of the God who originates all. If we can really face up to what we want, we want nothing less than reality itself, being itself, the why of it all, to be our friend and we his/hers. We want reality to be a loving self.

It is interesting to contrast this approach with another, very famous theological attempt to describe God in terms of human need—Paul Tillich's. Everyone, said Tillich, has an 'ultimate concern' that underlies all his/her motivation. Tillich's intention is to show this 'ultimate concern' to be God. But I don't think he ever succeeds in doing so. Why should our 'ultimate concern' be 'the Creator of Heaven and Earth', 'the source of the nature of things', 'what all call God'? There is no reason, *unless* we can show *in* the ultimate concern, in the ultimate anxiety, in the ultimate care/hope/wish/despair, in the ultimate loneliness, a desire for a companion whose description *is* the description of God. And this we do by insisting that we want one who is 'our lover in the nature of things', who therefore has to be the *source* of the nature of things.

In sum. What we need, and are perhaps in sight of, is a description of God out of human need that is clearly describing 'what all call God'.

Defining God by human need: 3

Let me try to pull together the attempt to define God by human need.

Can there be one who ends this ineluctable inner loneliness? Well, what is the ratio of this loneliness? It is: that I am, and nobody cares. But who could care that I am, but one by whose care I am? Is this just an Augustinian flourish? No, the ache in 'I am' is a seemingly meaningless constitutedness. The ultimate loneliness is to be constituted, without meaning, to be 'thrown into the world' as Sartre puts it. It throbs in all the drama of today. It underlies all the conflict of today.

'One by whose care I am' is identical with 'what all call God'. But this is still cold comfort. And the centre of the self, like the centre of the earth, is fire. The other who would lift me out of my inner loneliness would have to be not merely *the cause* for my exist- ence, but *by nature* and *of its essence* concerned with my existence. For the centre of the lonely 'I am' is an infinite insecurity generating an infinite narcissism. Somehow 'reality' must be 'for me', even 'for my sake'. This is the nature of the loneliness I am concerned with. Only the deeper spirits like Nietzsche touch it, but after him we may all feel it. Those who do not go that deeply may settle for a trusting theism—'one by whose care I am'—or a nonchalant athe- ism. But those who know what Eliot called the essential sickness and strength of the human soul have the terrible honesty to confess to the need for a reality that, if it ceased to think of me, would cease to exist; and either to decide such a reality impossible and decline into nihilism, as Nietzsche did, or to believe. And the content of *their* belief would be 'one who is the thought of me, subsisting'. It would be 'the intention of my being, embracing me'. It would be 'the idea of me being, alive'. And again—but this time much more closely to the heart's desire for the ache to end—'*the idea* of being, as *itself* being' is a tolerable paraphrase of Aquinas' *ipsum esse subsistens*, his favourite description of God which he got from an Arab.

The lonely heart desires that there be *ipsum esse subsistens*, that being be person, be friend. The meaning of loneliness is that being is not personal, not friend. For being is the human being's climate. Alone of all beings on earth, the human knows that he/she is and that everything is. Alone of all things, the human knows this, and the essence of loneliness is to perceive being without a face, without direction or purpose. For the inner self no longer lonely, the following monologue is appropriate—it is the heart's version of *ipsum esse subsistens*: 'The idea of my being *is*. It is "someone". It is will. It is eternal. That is why I am not doomed to be lonely, not doomed flatly and meaninglessly to be.'

The loneliness of being looks to the live idea of being as to its only possible companion. But if the possible makes itself actual for me, then, far from having the 'only refuge' quality that this language implies, the companion reveals an overwhelming beauty. The desperately needed becomes the infinitely desirable—and here indeed is the supreme and exemplary instance of one of the great rules of human being: that need has to translate itself into the generosity of desire, the supreme translator being Jesus, who said that his *food* was to do the will of the one who sent him. The ratio of this beauty is that the *idea* of being cannot be lonely and self-questioning but must be self-convinced and joyful. Once we permit our minds to entertain the thought of God, all parsimony is at an end. God is the eternal hedonist. For God is being, pleased with itself. It is almost impossible for our culture to admit this thought, since it has canonized loneliness to an unprecedented degree. God is *the* counter-cultural idea, *the* denial of loneliness and solemnity. As Eckhart puts it, 'God enjoys himself and want us to join him.' The live idea of my being, far from being a mere refuge from loneliness, invites me into his eternal dance.

In other words, the one who alone ends my ineluctable inner loneliness is the one *in* whom there is no loneliness. We naturally think of lonely people getting together so as to cease being lonely, but we also know that this never works, that what *looks* like 'it working' is a triumph, *in* each, of life over loneliness. What we are reflecting on in these pages is this triumph in its essence: the triumph of life over loneliness in a person through the coming into his or her life of the one *in* whom there is no loneliness, no self-questioning, no hesitancy: namely the live idea of being, the living reason for that person's existence.

Shared loneliness is far from being the remedy for loneliness; indeed the thing that finalizes our inner loneliness is precisely that it is shared. We all share it, which means that we cannot bring each other out of it. Only one can do this who knows nothing of loneliness, whom being, far from problematizing, totally satisfies. And thus the real pain of the inner loneliness is not 'I am, and no one cares' but 'I am, and no one dances'.

Finally, the whole thing can be condensed into the following syllogism:

> Existence unintended is the greatest conceivable loneliness, and the greatest conceivable loneliness desires the greatest conceivable relationship;
> therefore the greatest conceivable relationship is with that which intends my existence;
> but that which intends existence is what all call God;
> therefore the human being desires above all to be in love with God.

Note that this argument radically excludes the 'me and God and forget the rest' type of piety. 'The rest' is part of my loneliness. The rest *is* my loneliness. The awfulness of this loneliness shows itself precisely in the fact that all share it, none can relieve it.

The third pointer—mystical prayer

The most interesting thing about some recent off-the-cuff descriptions of 'the God I'd like there to be', obtained from a theology class, is this. Many of them stress the 'invisibility' (in the broadest sense) of God, and would like a God far more 'visible', more available to common experience, than God appears to be. In the ordinary way of things, we have little or no evidence of God at work in the world. As Woody Allen puts it in 'Love and Death', God is not dead, he's just an under-achiever! And the complaint at God's silence is found all through the psalms.

Now the thing we most want God for, the thing we most want there to be, is a reality that combines, nay identifies, 'its own being' with 'being-for me', or 'otherness' with 'for-me-ness', or 'being' with 'lovingness'. Now the fascinating thing about our complaint that God is not more 'visible' is that if he were, if we could take him in our mental 'sights', he would *not* be this strange being that equates being with being-for, because this identity, which we passionately and desperately *desire* to be a reality, is inconceivable to us! We *only* perceive lovingness in definite people who have plenty of interests other than ourselves. The 'lovingness' that is not such a quality *in* a person but is the very *being* of the person—that is right off the scale. But we want it!

What this means is that our clamour for God to be more visible and our heart's hunger for God *contradict each other*, pull in opposite directions. The heart wants a God that the mind cannot grasp, and if the mind could grasp him the heart would lose interest. All that the mind can do—and we've been doing this, and it's very important—is to say that this companion, in whom 'being' and 'being-for-me' are identical, is that incomprehensible reality that all call God.

The immensely popular movie 'Oh God', starring George Burns, brought out this contradiction, though I think without intending to.

God becomes visible to the young man, and thus satisfies the *first*, invisibility complaint. But in doing so he totally frustrates the *second*, and fundamental, requirement that the heart makes. How can George Burns be, or represent, one who is at once 'himself' and 'the thought of me'? George Burns has a life of his own. He faces a shaving-mirror. George Burns as God is far more incredible than *ipsum esse subsistens*, which we have rendered 'being-itself as someone'.

But can this be the end of the matter? Precisely, is God's reality given to the heart but only as a desire seemingly without object, and to the mind but only as the capacity to say why God cannot be conceived or imagined? Is there no availability of God to the mind *as something known*, as a reality met with? In other words, is there *no* 'visibility', no cognitive availability, of God? Is the complaint about God's invisibility absolutely without foundation? *Could* God, *can* God be more 'visible' to us?

The answer of religious tradition—of all religious traditions—is an emphatic yes. The mystical life, that grows like a vigorous plant in every religious soil, has developed ways of *so* quieting and disciplining our awareness that the reality of the inner companion begins to be 'evident', perceptibly to *attract*.

In other words, there are not only the hunger of the inner loneliness and the intellectual definition of God as an inconceivable identity of being with love. There is also a *faculty*, a *capacity* in the human mind to *become aware* of the mysterious reality that grounds all being and companions the heart.

In other words, between the *desire* for something that is inconceivable and the *idea* that enables us to see *why* it is inconceivable, there is a disciplined 'thinking about nothing' that is an opening of the heart-mind to this inconceivable beauty.

The existence of this 'third way' is a very powerful argument for the reality of 'the inner companion'—for the following reasons. One, it is astonishingly similar in all its different religious cradles; it is trans-cultural in other words. Thomas Merton, a Trappist monk from the modern West, found himself able to share his meditation experience with Buddhist monks and many others, including the Dalai Lama. Of course this is only an argument, not a proof. But it is a strong one. People who practise this type of inner concentration/relaxation not only are totally convinced *themselves* of a burning, all-loving reality beyond time and place; they *describe* the experience of this reality in language that is minimally tied to the time and place of their respective cultures.

The possibility that there is such a capacity or faculty in us is awakening growing interest today. People of many professions, of many beliefs and of no religious belief, are exploring a consciousness that, far from ceasing when the normal input of sensation ceases, seems to become more alive. Our culture is beginning to escape from its iron cage of materialism and rationalism. Of course it's a far cry from observing that there is an awareness of this kind to believing that God is. But once the fact of this awareness is recognized, the question comes up, 'What's it for?' Like the inner loneliness, it asks to be accounted for.

Finally, if this capacity finds expression in all cultures and seems able to transcend culture in the way it expresses itself, we have reason to suppose that something so simple, strong and universal is a capacity in all of us. The people we recognize as mystics are the people in whom this spark in all of us has managed to become a brilliant flame. I know that there are many, many mystics 'out there', unrecognized even perhaps by themselves.

PART ONE

Exploring the Inner Loneliness

Section Two

What is selfishness?

Self-love and self-gift easily go out of their natural alignment and come into conflict. The pain of this conflict between two equally valid and personal forces causes one of the parties to the conflict to be repressed. Certainly in childhood, where the foundations for future behaviour are laid, the claim of the other is much stronger than self-love is, imposing as it does the deadly fear of being rejected if one does not comply; so, self-love is the party that gets repressed.

Self-love unrepressed presents itself to the other without fear and asks for relationship, seeks to combine, to work-with, and this generates security. Self-love repressed, unacknowledged, unshared generates insecurity, a certain unease, a need to have everything and everyone my own way. It has often been remarked that it is *insecurity* that seeks power over others. The insecurity in question is what I have when, hiding my self-love from others and from myself, I retreat into myself and feel cut off, isolated. It is self-love, recognized and not repressed, that is my vital link, my connecting-point, with others, and security grows with this connection. As the link *weakens*, through the repression of self-love, security diminishes and this insecurity can only 'right itself' by getting power over others, by 'pulling the world my way'.

This need to control others has another important quality. It isn't like our 'straight' needs—for pleasure, for appreciation, for skills. These needs find 'straight' expression in *desires* which I know, acknowledge and freely satisfy. But the need to dominate has a *compulsive*, as opposed to a free quality. The person says to himself, not 'I *wish* to have everything my own way' but 'I've *got* to have everything my own way'. It is a dictated need. And the reason is that it is coming not from my 'conscious' but from my 'unconscious' mind, whither I have banished my self-love. Actually instead of Freud's 'conscious' and 'unconscious' I prefer to speak of the 'spoken'—to myself of course—and the 'unspoken' mind, of recognized and unrecognized desires. An 'unconscious desire' is simply a contradiction in terms.

Freud's most important discovery was that a person could experience such a conflict among his/her feelings that the socially unacceptable desire (e.g. to kill my father, to sleep with my mother) was pushed right down into the deep, unrecognized mind, whence it dictated totally irrational fears and behaviour patterns. This is the *extreme* case of 'control from the unknown mind', of crazy behaviour, and it's not what we're talking about here. But I want to suggest that what Freud was onto was the extreme, pathological *form* of a process that works less powerfully over a much wider area. And I think there is always something *a bit* 'mad' about our self-centred behaviour. It has been well said that the egoist is an enigma to himself. He doesn't really know *what* he's promoting.

For this is the kind of thing that self-centred, or selfish behaviour is. It is not a straight 'I want, I desire this'. It comes from something in myself that is just out of my reach and that wants to pull people and events my way. It is 'out of reach', because it is repressed self-love. Hence the profound observation of Austin Farrer, that the person doing evil never says to himself 'I want this' but something like 'this is what I do, must do'.

It is this 'dictated' quality of self-centred behaviour that gives rise to the insight, central to Paul's thought and also John's, that sin is an unfree thing, an enslavement. We freely *succumb* to it, but *it*, its dynamic, is not free. And while we're on Paul, one of his most important discoveries fits rather well into my theory of self-centred behaviour as repressed-self-love-dictated. The discovery was this—and it shocked Paul deeply, piously brought-up Jew that he was: that the Law—yes even the Holy Law of God—and sin were *on the same side*, both enemies of the human being.

The conflict between self-love and other-connection forces self-love underground whence it dictates desperate selfish behaviour. So anything that intensifies the conflict intensifies the repression and thus increases the selfish tendency that the repression produces. But the Law of God powerfully reinforces the claim of *the other*, the neighbour, society, family, *against* self-love. This intensifies the conflict which drives self-love underground to its devious launching pad. So the Law lends vigour to the very sinfulness it is trying to prevent! What is the way out? asks Paul. Only the new life in Jesus Christ and the Spirit—but how *this* way works must wait till later.

You'll find Paul's thought, in this matter of Law and sin, in the Letter to the Romans, especially chapters 7 and 8.

Thus everyone experiences two forms of the central desire: the desire to relate—stemming from unrepressed self-love—and the desire to control—stemming from repressed/unavowed self-love. And unrepressed self-love is healthy self-love, repressed self-love unhealthy self-love. An important conclusion follows. People are not *naturally* self-centred; that is not their natural, healthy functioning. They are *unnaturally*—but of course very prevalently—self-centred; that is their unnatural, unhealthy functioning.

Confusion here is fatal for theology—and very frequent. It is fatal, because once you see the self as naturally self-centred, you deny that the self wants God above all things, and you degrade God from being the fulfiller, the lover, into being the policeman. Paul's conversion, through the stunning vision of Jesus he had on the road to Damascus, was from God the policeman to God the lover. Self-love, repressed, turns to self-hatred, for I must hate the 'self' that is enslaving me. Theodore Isaac Rubin, psychiatrist, finds that all his patients suffer from self-hatred. There's a lot of it in us.

Finally, the universally experienced split between self-love and self-gift, whose ramifications we have been examining, is that more radical sense of guilt that has been an abiding concern of my work. Deeper than the sense of failing another, this radical or generic guilt feels an original non-alignment *between* self-love and self-gift, the non-alignment that *leads* to the choice of self against other.

49

What underlies the split between self-love and self-gift?

To attribute all the evil in our mutual dealings to a split between self-love and self-gift is to ask whence this split, in its turn, derives. The answer, I believe, lies in a split *within* self-love, which is most vividly experienced in the area of sexuality. This is the split between *desire*—heavily reinforced when sexual experience begins—and the need for *control*—heavily reinforced, in its turn, in reaction to the newly awakened desire.

This consideration sends us off on what may appear to be a vast digression—until our sexual experience appears to us as awakening in us *that* loneliness which we cannot relieve in each other, that loneliness which we have met already, which only God can relieve. Then our chain of causality for evil is complete—at least in the area of our sexuality which is, after all, our *erotic* experience of creature-hood. The chain is as follows. The inner loneliness, unrelieved, puts us at odds with our sexuality (and, as we shall see, with the other two great forms of our creaturehood, earth-dependence and mortality). Thus at odds with ourselves sexually, thus split between desire and control, we are split between self-love and self-gift.

With this goal of discovery in mind, the reader is invited to embark on an apparent digression on what is, on universal submission, an enthralling topic.

A word on incest

We have been thinking about the split, within self-love, between desire and control. Actually, it would be more accurate to speak of the new experience of desire as triggering a fear of *losing* control, of being out of control. This fear, most psychologists agree, is an important factor in sexual experience. Now we're going to take a rather strange path. I am going to suggest how we may account historically for this fear of losing control in the area of sexuality.

Here, first, is a fact that may surprise us. In all primitive societies, the strongest of all the tabus is the tabu on incest, sexual relations with sibling or parent or son or daughter. This surprises us civilized people, because the existence of a strong prohibition means the existence of a strong temptation, and the overwhelming majority of civilized people, far from being tempted by the thought of sexual intimacy with immediate kin, are repelled by it.

I have long been convinced that an important ingredient in theology is a good understanding of the vast difference between early and civilized society. So let's try to re-create a scenario in which incest would be tempting. Imagine sexual self-awareness growing in a young boy or girl *without* any mechanism operating to *divert* the new interest away from the bodies that are the closest and most familiar. Is it not just conceivable that in these circumstances it would be precisely the familiar, known and thus unthreatening bodies that would appear to offer the best outlet for this new and unknown desire?

No sooner has the incestuous desire surfaced than it encounters the tabu. Now there is a radical distinction between repression and restriction. Restriction means recognizing honestly that I desire something, and deciding that the prosecution of this desire is not appropriate; whereas repression means pretending to myself I don't have the desire. Now tabu is the most powerful form of restriction. It is restriction motivated by the belief that the forbidden object is

51

holy. The *reason* I must not enter the forbidden territory is that it is holy—and that is a very powerful reason. The word tabu has the same root as the word tapui, to make holy. Primitive society *hallows* the forbidden area and *thus* protects it from trespass.

But why should the idea of sexual relations within the nuclear family be holy? The reason is connected with what has already been said about their *desirability*. For in such relations, you have the co-presence of the two elements that make for a whole, fulfilling, creative sexual relationship, namely *passion* and *friendship*—the two elements which our society has the greatest difficulty in getting together. The incestuous union, though biologically undesirable—and the primitive knew this intuitively—does unite the two vital elements. The effect of the tabu is, all at once, to *remove* the incestuous union from the area of the permissible, and to *maintain* it before the mind's eye as a symbol of sexual wholeness, uniting passion with friendship, *hieros gamos*, the royal union. Possessed of this symbol, this archetype, the young primitive could then venture forth into the more threatening world of intimacy beyond the family circle. The tabu'd, hallowed object would reign at the centre of the mind and send the person out into inter-family relationships. The 'sending out' would be at once a sending—which is positive, 'go with my blessing!'—and a banishing, the negative side.

Now whereas the primitive boy or girl has his/her nascent sexual awareness placed and socially recognized, in other words made sense of, by the incest tabu; whereas these children get it connected from the start with the friendly familial world, the modern boy and girl stumble on their sexuality as a purely private event, a new and powerful force erupting within and having no connection, apparently, with the already familiar world of brothers and sisters and parents. Whereas in the nature of things—in the primitive state—the most interesting penis is one's father's and brothers,' the most interesting vagina one's mother's and sisters,' for the civilized boy or girl *these* genitalia are removed from view—and *not* by tabu but by repression. Here indeed we see most vividly the difference between tabu and repression. Sexual feeling, deprived of its friendly familiar mirror to validate itself in, is repressed, forced underground whence it exerts that compulsive, tyrannical power which, we have seen, characterizes *all* repressed desire.

A recent conversation brought home to me the difference between the primitive and the civilized. A friend recalled an early experience of looking up inside his mother's skirt and being smacked by the embarrassed parent. Now in a primitive family, we fantasized, the mother would have taken him on her knee that night, produced the totem pole, and told him the story enshrining the tabu. The effect of this on the boy would be to give him a sense of growing up, being recognized, entering into the experience of the tribe. It would give him status. Whereas what my friend encountered made him feel small, somehow dirty. It drove him into his private self, there to handle alone what once was handled by the whole tribe.

It is sexual desire in this privatized form, coming from this unknown (Freud's 'unconscious') place, that generates the fear of losing control and thus sets up *between* desire and control the tension which we are currently investigating.

If you enjoy massive oversimplification, as I do, you may say that the whole emotional sickness of the West, from the Pope downwards, lies in the replacement of the incest tabu by sexual repression. But then it may be asked: if our desire-control split is simply the result of losing touch with our primitive side, how are you going to maintain that it is due to being out of touch *with God?*

Just to sketch an answer to this huge question. Granted that the primitive does not suffer the desire-control split, he has this harmony only because he has not developed the many sides of the human potential. The things that are in us only come into tension as we grow. There is no tension in the uninflated balloon, growing tension as we inflate. Just as it is ruinous to *ignore* the primitive in us—psychoanalysis is, I think, the attempt to restore it to us—it is ruinous to disavow the civilized. The human being *is* in growth. And the civilization that exchanged tabu for repression built the cathedrals and made possible the soaring mind of Augustine and Aquinas. And so we *can* see the deep tensions in us that our development has revealed, as symptomatic of the most fundamental unease of all, our unease with the huge, mysterious yet personal force in which we 'live and move and have our being', as Paul puts it. And I shall shortly be arguing that we don't like sex because we don't know God. This principle can be illustrated by the following story.

Oedipus Rex

Note the sequence of events in this tale. First, the *parents* are warned by the Oracle that their son will kill his father and marry his mother. They try to *dodge* the tabu by eliminating the son. But the son survives and is adopted by the King and Queen of Corinth, whom he grows up thinking to be his parents. Then *the son* is warned by the Oracle that he will kill his father and marry his mother. He, too, tries to *dodge* the tabu by running away. But in flight he encounters, unknowingly, his real father, gets drawn into a quarrel and kills him. He then goes on to his real home, Thebes, falls in love with the bereaved Queen, unknowingly his real mother, and seeks her hand. He then solves the riddle of the Sphinx, thus saving the young of the city. Acclaimed as saviour, he marries Jocasta and reigns for sixteen years until Tiresias the seer exposes to him his terrible crime. Thereupon he blinds himself, and Jocasta kills herself.

Thus, in spite of the attempt both of parents and of child to dodge it, the tabu lures him into its snare so that he breaks it unwittingly and incurs its terrible revenge. So in this tragedy the tabu is no longer the beneficent force it was in primitive society, but is a cruel, malevolent fate that lures its victim into its trap. The tabu has become a sort of Catch-22.

What is the significance of this change in the incest tabu from creative symbol to malicious trap? Many scholars are arguing today that the tragedy *Oedipus Rex* is the response to a very profound shift in the organization of society.[1] The reason why the incest tabu ceases to work as a centring, balancing force and becomes a curse is that it is part of a whole way of life which is coming to an end.

---

[1] Oedipus stands at the crucial point in history which Jaspers has called the first axial shift, the birth of a new, universal human consciousness. It is the period of the great Greek tragedies and of the great Hebrew prophets. Jaspers believed that we are experiencing a second axial shift.

That way of life was 'simple', by which one means that the goals pursued by society were not far *beyond* the goal of the good life *of* society. It is this *growing distance* between intellectual, economic and political adventure on the one hand, and the well-being of the family on the other, that is the hallmark of what we call civilization. With Oedipus Rex we are really at the beginning of civilization, of the new way.

There is another very important characteristic of the earlier stage where the family and its good are paramount. It is woman-controlled, matriarchal. In the incest tabu, it is the mother who controls. The incest tabu is women teaching men how to become men. They decree the ritual, central to which is the incest tabu. By the tabu, the man is led by the mother beyond herself into the larger life of the tribe.

According to the theory we are now examining, *Oedipus Rex* marks the massive turnover from this matriarchal society to the new patriarchal society, in which man conquers new domains of territory and spirit, and pays the price of having to work out his sexual identity by himself instead of learning it from the mother-controlled tribe. Oedipus stands at this turning-point. The 'old way' unleashes all its force against him to hold him captive. He accepts its terrible punishments, but then, self-blinded, he sets out on the way of inner enlightenment and self-discovery. Oedipus is the first 'modern' man; and it is not for nothing that he has given his name to what all more or less agree to be the most important of our growth crises, the conquest of male and female identity in a society based *on* personal identity and no longer on tribal solidarity.

All the indications are that this new patriarchal age is itself reaching its end in our time. There is hardly a crisis in our time that does not reduce to being unhappy with ourselves, with each other, and with our earth. And this is the lot of man the adventurer, Oedipal man, as he steps out of the 'psychic womb' of the women-controlled tribe onto the path of endless discovery. An age comes to an end when its liabilities hugely outweigh its assets.

A third age is dawning, whose form is still very unclear to us. The patriarchal age of sexual repression, which succeeded the matriarchal age of tribally taught sexuality and the incest tabu, is giving way to a new control by feminine wisdom, far deeper and more universal than the old matriarchy, *combining* the naturalness of the latter with the spirituality of the patriarchal age.

What *is* the meaning of our sexuality? The first answer was that

55

it is a mystery into which we are tribally initiated under maternal auspices. The second answer was that it was a theme for personal self-discovery by men (Oedipus breaking free of the old tabu-structure) with women as helpers (the dominance of man succeeding the dominance of woman). The third answer is that at the end of the road of self-discovery taken by Oedipus there is only our relatedness to God, in whose 'Kingdom' man and woman are part of each other, the model of dominance giving way at last to that of friendship. This is the 'third age' prefigured by Jesus. In the end the problem of sexuality, of an existence at once spiritual and earthbound, is the problem of God. Only in the experience of being-created can we be totally at one with our sexuality. It may have taken all these millenia to discover this truth.[2]

I am suggesting that we shall not be at one with ourselves as sexual beings until we come into a new experience of our createdness. We have already seen that it is only the God who *is* 'the thought of us' who can break open our ineluctable loneliness. And is not the very sense of our loneliness the feeling of being a spirit adrift on the vast impersonal sea of matter? And does not our sexual self-awareness bring this dual condition into the strongest focus? Thus 'the ending of our inner loneliness' and 'becoming at one with ourselves sexually' are two sides of the same coin. When Augustine said, 'Our heart is restless till it rests in Thee', he could equally have said, 'Spirit and flesh in us are ill-at-ease with each other until we rest in Thee'. As we contemplate the (to us) strange ritual of the incest tabu, and the anguish of Oedipus inaugurating our own endless sexual problematic, we sense our life to be founded in one in whom alone we can fully live.

---

[2] Once we see that it is only through a wholly new spiritual maturity, a new aliveness to the transcendent one, that we can be at one with ourselves sexually, we can understand the bind the medieval Church was in. The medieval Church firmly *believed* that spirit and flesh are both of God and both 'very good', as Genesis says. But its *behaviour* told a different story. The Church treated sexuality as though it were evil. It did not have the more mature *experience* of God-the-Creator through which *alone* it is possible to hold flesh and spirit together *in practice*. Thus you get the paradox that the Church vehemently denounced the dualistic *doctrine* ('theory') while behaving ('praxis') as though that doctrine were true.

Sexual identity: 1

The main point of the Oedipus tragedy is this. Oedipus seeks to know who he is, his meaning and destiny as a man. And he seeks to know this, *not* from the tribal wisdom that shunts him from the tabu'd incest to a functional mating, but *from within*. At this crucial stage in psychic history, self-awareness has become intense enough to pull away from the 'psychic womb' of tribal wisdom; and in pulling away, he has only himself to draw on for his male identity, its emotional meaning. His self-blinding symbolizes a commitment to the hazardous inward search.

Let me say at once that the story concerns masculine identity, the more or less successful pursuit of which characterizes the whole of the patriarchal age, and that the corresponding search, by woman, for *her* identity has been delayed right into our time and indeed is characteristic of the 'third age'. One cannot overestimate the importance of this feat of feminine self-discovery; it is as massive as has been the Oedipus revolution. Thus most of the talk we hear today, from men and women, to the effect that man and woman are *complementary*, is bland talk still within the patriarchal mindset. It is, in fact, Oedipal man saying to woman, 'Now I've established myself, I want you as my complement'. Much more is involved in woman's self-discovery.

Back to Oedipus then. He symbolizes the breakdown of all man's *external* sources for self-knowing. He consults the Oracle, and what he gets from the Oracle is not wisdom but a dirty trick. So he has to seek within.

Now the point I want to make is this. In experiencing myself as a man, I know I am only half of the human whole. And the natural conclusion would be that it is only with a woman that I can know myself as man, as the 'male half' of the whole. But there is *something more* about my masculine identity that I cannot learn in this way, just as there is something more about a woman's self-awareness that she cannot learn with a man. That 'something more', that core-identity, is what Oedipus has to go in search of.

Now this sense of having to seek *within* myself the meaning of what I perceive 'without' as maleness—sex characteristics and so on—is *lonely*. It is *the* loneliness of the human, the cosmic orphan, whom nature tells so much about himself and then goes silent. It is the loneliness to which Oedipus commits himself as he steps away from the tribe and ancient ways. And clearly it is a loneliness that nobody and nothing outside himself can alleviate.

And we have met it before. For what is the loneliness that no other can alleviate, if not the 'inner loneliness'? Therefore the loneliness of the male in search of identity (as of the female) is a yearning for that 'one who is the thought of me' that 'all call God'.

Now men, in our patriarchal period, have partly understood this—but only partially. They have found their male identity, beyond the woman, in God; but they have misunderstood this experience: they have made God male and used him to endorse their dominance over woman. This is extraordinarily and by now embarrassingly clear, in the Vatican attitude to sexuality as evidenced in the 1981 Roman synod on the family. Maybe it is only in the 'third age', when women too are seeking their identity transcendentally and beyond man, that women *and* men will learn to find themselves in God without reducing God to themselves, male or female.

The split, within the man and within the woman, between male and female, is a loneliness that only God can heal. Certainly it is only in the mind of God that man and woman are one; but our inner loneliness yearns to be touched by that mind. You see the enormous importance, for a radical understanding of sexuality, of establishing that the inner loneliness that is the core of human self-awareness is a craving for that mysterious reality 'that all call God'. Everything radical in the human, his/her sexuality, his/her earth-dependence, his/her mortality, *is* that loneliness in search of its unimaginable friend.

Once we understand this divine source of sexual identity, we can become aware of something in the Genesis myth of the creation of man and woman that we easily miss, though it is quite obvious. It is *not* the story of man and woman and their complementarity, with God as the mere architect or mechanic or inventor. It is the story of man and woman and God. It is the emotional story of man and woman and God. God creates first not a man (*ish*) but an undifferentiated human (*Atham*—Adam), sees it is lonely and splits it into man (*ish*) and woman (*isha*). The meaning is, that they will find their meaning in each other but only provided they find the meaning of their respective 'halving' of the human whole in God.

In other words, the principle already enunciated that 'the other within changes the other without' applies intimately to the union of the sexes, which otherwise is limited to a functional complementarity that can satisfy the hunger of neither. To the man who is finding God within himself, the woman is not just a mysterious other-half but a person anchored in the eternal. And the same applies of course to the vision of him that she is to have.

Theology will begin to be doing its job when 'God' connotes that wine without which life is tepid water. It is far short of this stage as yet.

Sexual identity: 2

As the thought in that last chapter is rather compact, I am setting it out here in a more structured form, as a series of logical steps.

1. Oedipus. Leaves the tribe, and must search within for the meaning of his manhood.

2. Why must a man seek within for the meaning of his manhood? Surely manhood, womanhood, is a function of mating, not something to be discovered within?

3. No, and this is crucial. A person's manhood, or womanhood, is the completion of his or her *identity*. In the beginning I was 'will'. Then—age two to four—I was 'person'. Then, with what Freud calls the Oedipal phase, I am 'a man' or 'a woman'. Therefore, since my sex is my complete *identity*, I must seek its meaning within.

4. At the same time, I cannot but *contrast* manhood, which is mine, with womanhood. This contrast with woman, the visible other, the visibly different, is obviously a vital part of my identity as a man.

5. But there is something about my male identity that this contrast does not show me. It shows me that I am not complete, that I only, as it were, realize *half* of human nature. *But it does not tell me the meaning of this incompleteness.*

6. In rather the same way, the world tells me that I am mortal, but it does not tell me the *meaning* of my mortality, and the earth tells me that I am dependent, but it does not tell me the *meaning* of my dependence.

7. This condition, of being told of my incompleteness by the other sex, of my mortality by the world, and of my dependence by the earth, while all these *remain silent* as to my inner meaning, is the condition of *loneliness*: the loneliness of the cosmic orphan, whom nature tells so much about himself and only so much. This is the loneliness that impels us to search within. It is a loneliness which, by definition, nobody and nothing outside myself can alleviate.

8. AND WE HAVE MET IT BEFORE. It is the 'inner loneliness'. It is the hunger of the human heart for 'the one who is the thought of me.'

9. Therefore it is to 'the one who is the thought of me' that I am directed in my search for *sexual* identity.

10. Thus the search for sexual identity goes *beyond* the other sex to the other who gives me identity as a man.

11. Now we can look at history. The search for identity, after release from the tribal oneness, is at first a male search. This is the patriarchal age whose croaking is now audible. In this period— especially exemplified in the Church Fathers (there were not Church Mothers, alas!) and the Middle Ages—man as monk or knight or whatever finds his identity in God beyond woman. The experience, though real, is distorted. Man indeed 'finds his male identity in God' *literally*, finds God male and uses this God to endorse his dominance over woman. But badly distorted though it thus is, there *is* some experience of the male identity beyond woman, in the beyond that is God. The Oedipal project.

12. In the 'third age', woman is to find *her* identity beyond man, in the beyond that is God. This is a revolution as massive as has been the Oedipal revolution. It will create a whole new philosophy, political and economic, new ways of thinking, of settling disputes, of healing.

13. We often hear it said that man and woman are complementary. This is true so far as it goes, but it does *not* speak to the crucial problem of a man's and a woman's identity. When it *is* addressed to the identity-problem, it is either a man saying to the woman, 'You are complementary *to me*', or vice versa. Probably the former, since man has been culturally at the centre for so long. This attitude is simply patriarchalism thinly disguised.

14. Re-read the Genesis creation story. It is not the story of man and woman with God as the mere designer or producer. It is the story of man and woman and God. It is the emotional story of man and woman and God. In it God creates not 'a man' (*ish*) but undifferentiated humanity (*Atham*—Adam), sees it is lonely and splits it—the rib story—into *ish* and *isha*. So the very distinction and complementarity of man and woman is seen as something of which God is the secret meaning. Man and Woman are to find their meaning in each other, but they will only do so in finding their respective meaning in God.

15. When women today, as they increasingly do, complain, 'I

am not recognized as a woman', they are not satisfied when men reply, 'but surely we are complementary to each other'. And rightly so. What they are giving expression to is the *woman's* identity-search, which is as momentous historically as was the man's, which is as much oriented as is the man's to 'the other who is the thought of me'.

16. The principle that 'the other within changes the other without' applies most intimately to the union of the sexes. A man who is finding God within himself sees his wife as far more than his complement: he sees her as a person rooted in the eternal. And vice versa of course.

17. On these principles, we can have some understanding of celibacy. True celibates are rare—not in the sense of superior but in the sense that watchmakers are rare. They represent *one* of the *many* options that open up once we have restored the inner-companion dimension to sexuality: the option of finding one's sexual identity in God beyond the other sex (as all mature married people need to do) and *without* a committed union with one of the other sex.

18. The most important notion, on which all the above really depends, is that being a man or being a woman is the final basic identity of a person, and not a mere function of mating.

Sex and God

You may be wondering how our study of incest-tabu, Oedipus, the patriarchal age and the 'third age' (in quotes because it hasn't happened) connects with our search for the root of human evil. Here's a suggestion. We may compare the whole search to an exploration of caves—speleology or spelunking. We are working downwards in the human psyche, in search of the root of evil. At the surface we note the fact that all evil consists in people harming each other and themselves. Deeper, at the first plateau, we discover the immediate source of this universal evil—the coming-apart of self-love and self-gift, with the consequent repression of self-love so that it becomes a compulsive source of the power bid. But we do not discover, at this level, *why* self-love splits off from its full context of self-gift. For this we have to go deeper. We get our hint, our passageway, for this further descent, in the birth of sexual self-awareness, universally known as the loss of innocence: for there we can observe a crisis *within* self-love that would account for its morose withdrawal from the other. This crisis we called the new tension between desire and control.

Now until recently, I have tried to find a passageway from this ill-at-ease-ness with our sexuality to the still deeper level where the God-dimension appears. It wasn't easy, and I wasn't satisfied. Recently, the chance discovery of a book called *Incest and Human Love* by Robert Stein led me to realize that the 'sex-plateau' is much broader than I had thought. Before trying to go deeper, why not explore this plateau a bit more? Training our powerful lamps on the darkness, the cave proved to be vast. It proved to be, in fact, the whole history of sexuality and society! And what this history revealed is the slow emergence of *sexual identity* out of tribal consciousness; male sexual identity first, occupying pretty well the whole of civilized history so far, then female identity, threshholding a new age.

This idea of sexual identity needs explaining. Basically, the question of sexual identity is what emerges when self-awareness is sufficiently strong to interact with sexual function. The sexual function of the man is to impregnate the woman. And as long as we are in the tribal, matriarchal age, the man more or less gets his meaning from this function. 'More or less', because the receiving of the incest tabu is already a beginning of sexual identity. But—and this is the point—this sense of sexual identity is being *given* the young man *by* the tribe. *As* the sense of being 'simply myself and not the tribe's creation' grows, that sense fastens onto my sexuality and makes of *it* something the tribe cannot explain to me, makes of *it* something I must seek the meaning of within myself. And in point of fact, we all remember being intensely curious about ourselves sexually long before—almost another ten-year gap—we had any real understanding of our sexuality as functional to mating. That long period saw the building-up of sexual identity. In that period—certainly the earlier part—the boy sees the girl's body as 'a body *without* a penis' not as 'a body with its own type of organ'—that is, entirely with reference to himself, his own sexual being.

Now the delay at this plateau proved to have been worth it. For it is sexual identity that opens up the passageway to the deepest cave. How so? Because the question 'Who am I as a man?' is a question *provoked* by my body and by the body of the other sex, but not *answered* by either. And this condition, of getting no answer about myself from the world that puts up the questions of myself, is the cause of that deeper and essential loneliness of the human that we have met already. And so we have the passageway to the deepest level—the ultimate, ineluctable loneliness of being human that is only lifted by 'one who is the thought of me, one who thinks me'.

Also the penultimate cave reveals huge further extensions at this same point of sexual identity. For *just as* the fact of my sexuality and of the opposite sex provokes a question that these cannot answer—the question of my meaning, of my worth—so the fact of my participation in universal mortality provokes a question that it cannot answer, and similarly with the fact of my dependence on the earth for survival. So this cave turns out to be trefoil-shaped, featuring sexuality, mortality and earth-dependence, and these three emphasizing the question of my ultimate meaning *which I have to face alone*. And thus we arrive, by a far ampler route than I had realized before, at the deepest level of human self-awareness, which is the great loneliness that only one partner can relieve: the cosmic loneliness.

Baldly, then, loneliness unrelieved is the cause of sin, of all the evil and destructiveness in human-kind. The Christian tradition so far has not been sufficiently introspective to understand this principle. It has rooted sin, not in loneliness but in independence. Independence is a much simpler notion. It simply means wanting things my own way—and of course this desire is very strong in us. But loneliness is a desire *not* to be alone, not to have things my own way. In a heavy quarrel between spouses, one of them will angrily say, 'All right—have it your own way!', which really is a kind of excommunication: 'Be alone—be miserable!' Thus loneliness is a more radical, complex and human condition than independence. Unrelieved, it is that root of all human evil for which we are looking.

Relieved, of course, it is the source of all the good that we do. This same core loneliness in the human being is at once the potential for heroic sanctity and for the worst depravity. There is nothing in us that is the source of evil and of nothing else. There is no evil principle in the human being. The belief that there is is the oldest heresy with which the Church has had to contend—dualism—and with which the Church is always, in practice, somewhat tainted.

The reason why 'complementarity' is not the answer to the question about male and female sexual identity is that when we think of sexual identity we are thinking of the experience, by the sexes, of each other. We are not looking down on both from above and seeing the fit. In *that* perspective, complementarity is evident, not in the perspective of sexual identity.

The only thing that will bring the sexes together in that deep way that we so much desire, is the acceptance by each sex of its cosmic loneliness, and of the desire for God which this loneliness is.

Here is a poem by Matthew Arnold that treats our theme, though with characteristic Victorian pessimism. It is called 'Isolation'.

Yes! in the sea of life enisled,
With echoing straits between us thrown,
Dotting the shoreless watery wild,
We mortal millions live *alone*.
The islands feel the enclasping flow,
And then their endless bounds they know.

But when the moon their hollows lights,
And they are swept by balms of spring,

And in their glens, on starry nights,
The nightingales divinely sing;
And lovely notes, from shore to shore,
Across the sounds and channels pour—

Oh! then a longing like despair
Is to their farthest caverns sent;
For surely once, they feel, we were
Parts of a single continent!
Now round us spreads the watery plain—
Oh might our marges meet again!

Who ordered that their longing's fire
Should be, as soon as kindled, cooled?
Who renders vain their deep desire?
A God, a God their severance ruled!
And bade betwixt their shores to be
The unplumbed, salt, estranging sea.

Loneliness and the Garden

Loneliness is how I feel when the world is silent to my question 'Who am I?' There is loneliness in my sexual identity in that my body does not tell me who I am. There is loneliness in my mortality and in my earth-dependence, for in those areas too my question meets with silence.

The *result* of this loneliness, in the area of sexuality, is as follows. Since my sexuality, with its desires, does not answer my question of identity, I am ill-at-ease with it. To be lonely is to be 'up-tight'. And *because* I am ill-at-ease with my sexuality, I fear it, associate it with loss of control. Hence the tension, in civilized, highly self-aware man between desire and control. Hence also the difficulty of uniting friendship with passion: for if I do not befriend my sexuality, how can I give it in a friendly way to a partner? And how many of the tensions in marriage are due to this non-alignment between the easy give-and-take of two persons in ordinary concourse and the seemingly different dynamic of two persons in passion?

Thus the immediate effect of cosmic loneliness is ill-at-ease-ness with our sexuality. Self-consciousness, male and female, which is the experience of the sexual-identity problem, finds itself strangely at odds with the natural dynamic that draws them to one another.

This phenomenon is illustrated with power, beauty and simplicity in the Genesis myth of the Fall, which may be called the story of the beginning of cosmic loneliness. Adam and Eve break with the Companion, with the one who is the thought of them, and the immediate effect is discomfort with their bodies in each other's presence. Here is the account. 'She took some of the fruit and ate of it, and gave some to her husband and he ate of it, and immediately their eyes were opened and they saw that they were naked, and they made for themselves loincloths out of figleaves.' The point is reinforced later in the story. Adam and Eve hide from God and, when God asks them why they are hiding, Adam replies, 'I heard

67

your voice and hid because I was naked', *and God says*, 'Who told you you were naked?'

This story is of crucial importance for our self-understanding. The Christian tradition so far has misread this text. It has stated that the *immediate* consequence of the breach with God is disorder in the passions (lust in the case of sex). The text, however, clearly says otherwise. The *immediate* consequence is 'shame', ill-at-ease-ness with sexuality, so that what is no longer a *friend* becomes a *threat*. Sexuality is out of control *because* it is unbefriended, and this is the *meaning* of lust. In other words, shame generates lust, not lust shame. The tradition so far has had this the wrong way round.

The immediate consequence of loss-of-touch with God is not loss of *control* over sexual and other desires. It is loss of *friendship* with sexual and other desires. If a person can befriend his or her desires, control is not a problem: it is simply a part of being 'together'. On the other hand, the befriending of desire only comes about through coming *into* touch—in some way—with the Companion, out-of-touchness with whom causes the *un*befriending of desire. It is only when a person begins to come out of that loneliness of the male, or of the female—which makes him/her a problem to him/herself sexually and therefore not at ease with the opposite sex—that a person learns to befriend his or her natural inclination.

It is difficult for us, with the Christian tradition behind us the way it has thought so far, to think of God in this way, to realize that we don't like sex because we don't know God. (Please note that word 'like'. Of course we love sex, want sex, need sex, buy and sell sex and so on and on. But we're not *friendly* with it.) When John Paul II said that man is not the slave of passion, he voiced two thousand years of tradition. He spoke, in other words, out of the *struggle* of man (and his standpoint is very male) with a force in him that threatens to divert him from the quest for God and for justice in human relations. But if sexual desire is, for me, essentially a distraction from God, then my quest for God is nothing other than the male quest for his identity, which characterizes the patriarchal age, that lonely quest which makes him ill-at-ease with the (none-theless desired) sexual partner. So it all begins to fit together. The patriarchal age, the male preoccupation with his sexual identity, the consequent ill-at-ease-ness with sexual desire for the other (and I stress that you can be ill-at-ease with a desire that totally consumes you: that's *why* it totally consumes you!), the thinking of sexual passion as something which you will either master or be mastered by (as opposed to befriending and being befriended by)—all this is the civilized symptomatology of the condition so simply and beautifully portrayed in Genesis, the origin of cosmic loneliness. Animal sexuality is functional to mating and procreation. Human sexuality, while essentially unitive and procreative, is the response to a double loneliness, cosmic and personal.

I know whereof I speak, for I had an experience in which the God of the patriarchal tradition and the God of at-one-ness with our nature came into collision inside me: I mean, the God who is our ally in the struggle with sex and the 'lure of woman'—a recurrent theme of the patriarchal age—and the God who *originates* sex and all other pleasures. I was reading, for the umpteenth time, that passage in Genesis: 'They took the fruit, and immediately their eyes were opened and they saw that they were naked, so they made for themselves loincloths', and the word 'immediately' sprang out at me—so *that's* what it meant to lose God, it meant being ashamed of one's sex!—and I said, 'Good God! The God who said to Adam and Eve, "Who told you you were naked?", and the God I was brought up on who would damn you eternally for masturbating *are not on speaking terms*, are not the same God!' We have a split God. At this point in time, we can experience with special vividness this split between 'a God of control' and 'a God of desire', because we are at an axial shift, at the turnover from God as seen by the patriarchal age to God as he/she is trying to show him/herself now. What you are enduring in this book is a theologian trying to think in the axial shift: like watching someone climbing a greasy pole.

You see how our earlier thought on 'God the hedonist' comes in here. It is only now when we try to understand the condition of being *out of touch* with this original act of enjoyment that we can see the whole history of human sexuality as manifesting this out-of-touch-ness, the sexual dimension of the cosmic loneliness.

Of course the human condition is not *totally* 'out of touch'. If it were, it could not *feel* out of touch. That is why loneliness is such a good description of it. As I said before, independence means wanting nothing to do with the other, while loneliness is haunted by the other. And of course the God who 'haunts' me easily becomes the punishing, control-God of the patriarchal age.

Sexual identity and cosmic loneliness

The sense of sexual identity begins at about age five and is culturally reinforced during the succeeding decade. I learn to think of myself as a man or a woman: and that is how I think of *myself*—as a boy or as a girl. The *meaning* of being a man cannot be known until woman has come into the picture.

Now this is where the snag appears. It is this. The *attraction* towards woman (and all this is reversible of course), which begins to be strong in early adolescence, is clearly the 'coming of woman into the picture'. But it is experienced as a powerful force *in its own right* rather than as the filling-out of my understanding of myself as a man. (The incest tabu, we saw, connects it more with self-understanding than does the modern experience of growth, for it connects sexual attraction with the near familiars who have largely given me my sense of identity.) Far from telling me who I am, it further confuses me.

So that which would, in other circumstances, show me the full meaning of myself as a man does not do so. What would be those 'other circumstances'? An unimaginable *harmony* between my self-awareness/self-love and the force of nature, the dark force which 'puts the other sex in the picture' in the above lopsided way.

Now this harmony between self-awareness/self-love and the force of nature would be precisely the condition of *not* being the cosmic orphan. In other words, the 'perfect' union of man and woman can exist only in the condition where the cosmic loneliness is no more.

In the condition of the cosmic orphan, 'in this our exile' as the beautiful medieval prayer puts it, the search for male or female identity gropes in part towards God, in whose companionship alone it is to be found with woman, but in part reinforces male or female identity *against* the opposite sex and against nature.

The very copiousness of the evidence for male self-assertion, at this time of awakening female self-awareness, understandably leads feminists to *write off* the patriarchal age—unfortunately, for it involves the negating of that very historical process which now is beginning to make a momentous change in direction.

Some difficulty may be experienced with the assertion that the sexual identity quest 'gropes towards God'. What I mean is not an explicitly religious aspiration but a certain element or atmosphere of exaltation that can characterize the male quest for meaning—the one for which we have far more evidence for study so far. There is an *instinctive* feeling that sexual identity is involved in mystery. A striking example would be the exalted atmosphere that surrounds medieval knighthood, the all-night vigil of self-dedication (theme of innumerable Victorian paintings), the whole Arthurian legend, the quest for the Holy Grail. Wagner brilliantly popularized this medieval chivalry emotion, and his influence on Hitler and the Nazi movement was profound and fatal. Significantly, a widely acclaimed study, by a man, of male psychology—*He* by Robert A. Johnson—is an exposé of the myth of the Grail quest. Also significantly, a study of female psychology—*She* by the same author—using the myth of Psyche and Aphrodite, has been judged very inadequate by all the women I know who have read it. It is a patriarchal book, studying woman as seen by man. The *female* quest is something else. It looks ahead to the 'third age'.

Sex, God and the Church

It is surely necessary, at this time of rapid cultural shift, to attempt to get a wide-angle view of sexual morals and of the Church's presence in this sphere. So I want to share with you some thinking I have been doing recently, whose purpose has been to discover the connection, in experience, between sexuality and God. For the sake of clarity, we need to attempt some formulation of the fundamental problem of human sexuality. This may seem an oversimplifying approach, but perhaps it is worth attempting. I spoke of a wide-angle view, after all.

I have found, first, that a crucial concept is that of sexual identity. I accept as broadly true the Freudian belief that the main foundations of the person-to-be are laid by about age five. By then, the whole package is put together in a rudimentary way. We have already characterized the stages of this assembling as follows. From zero to one-plus, I was 'will'. From then to three-four, I was the beginning of a 'person'. Finally, around four-five, I was 'boy' or 'girl'. My sexual identity is the final and the fullest edition or version of myself, of what I am to think of myself as.

Sexual identity, once it emerges, is heavily endorsed by the culture's idea of what men and women are like. But it seems to me vital to be clear that the effect of the culture, though powerful and fateful, is to *interpret* the sexual difference, not to *create* it.

I have long wondered why sexual identity is so important and has always been thought to be so. The best reason I can come up with is that for all the scope of his or her mind, the human being is not independent but is woven into a whole continuum of nature. The points of contact for this interweave are dependence on the earth for sustenance, sexuality, and mortality. These provide, according to Northrop Frye, the only three universal human images: of food as sacred, of mating as sacred, and of life as a journey. They also provide, universally, the three themes of the so-called 'shadow language'—words that are only written on walls. Sustenance, sex and death are the three great reminders of our incompleteness, our fragility. But whereas need and death press indifferently on all persons, sex makes a difference between two sorts of persons. It makes a deeper inroad into personhood. It gets right into personhood, to name the person as one or the other half of the human whole. The reminder that men and women get of their incompleteness by looking at their body sexually is a subtler, deeper, and above all more emotionally involving reminder than that of the pangs of hunger and mortality.

Another thing has to be said, however, about the three reminders. They not only remind. They accentuate what I call a cosmic loneliness. For the self-aware being, alone in the cosmos, asks who he/she is. Self-awareness seeks a place to be, seeks to *have* a place, to belong, seeks for his/her meaning. And when, impelled thus to question, I ask *nature* who I am, nature is silent. This silence brings home to me that, at root, I am lonely. The human being, says Loren Eiseley, is the cosmic orphan.

Now let's put these two ideas together: that the three experiences of our interweaving with nature awaken in us a cosmic loneliness; and that, *of* these three experiences, the sexual makes the deepest inroad of nature into our *identity*. It follows from this conjunction that my sexual identity gives me an especially strong sense of cosmic loneliness.

The importance of this phenomenon is that my maleness looks not only to woman and to mating but to whatever it is that may speak to me where nature is silent. In other words, people are sexually involved with the lonely problem of God and meaning, and not only with each other contrasexually. The enormous cultural investment, in all cultures, in the assigning and endorsing of sex *roles*, is evidence of this powerful preoccupation in people with making sense of themselves *as* men, *as* women, quite apart from their complementarity in union. Popular psychology has given us all sorts of ideas of the different factors involved in sexual intimacy—such as 'that there are always at least four people in the bed'—but the most important thing to consider is that each of the parties is looking in two opposite directions: to the other, and within the self.

The 'two looks' are not at all easy to align. In fact, if we are to attempt a single answer to our opening question, 'What *is* the sexual problem?', it is here: how do we align passion with friendship? How

73

do we align sex as powerful attraction to another with sex as 'who I am', with sex as that 'final edition of personhood'?

My belief is that they are out of alignment *because* we are 'cosmic orphans'. Sexuality makes us lonely as well as drawing us to each other. This idea is simply and poignantly expressed in the story of the Fall, which might have been called 'How Cosmic Loneliness Began': 'She ate of the fruit and gave some to her husband and he ate. And immediately their eyes were opened, and they saw that they were naked. So they sewed for themselves loincloths out of figleaves.' The *immediate* effect of losing touch with God is the awkwardness of the sexes with each other, through the involvedness of *each* with his/her loneliness, with the lost God. And this awkwardness, this non-alignment, is the root of all our sexual disorders. The Christian tradition has been so much preoccupied *with* these disorders that it has seen *them* as the immediate consequence of the Fall. It has failed so far to understand that being out of touch with God means being *out of friendship* with my body and its desires, rather than being *no longer master* of my desires. Shame generates lust, not lust shame.

Now we must look at history. For if our cosmic loneliness entails an immense preoccupation of each sex with itself, our culture since the dawn of civilization has overwhelmingly emphasized the male quest for identity over the female. The male 'ideal-types'—of warrior, knight, monk, sage, king, priest—heavily predominate. If woman figures at all in the quest for identity, she is the seductress, the temptress, the witch, the siren who lures man off course and onto the rocks—man in search of his identity, his Holy Grail. This is the shape of the patriarchal age, which, according to some scholars, was originally a breakaway from a matriarchal age in which the 'non-alignment' was hardly felt because self-awareness was hardly present.

Now that gives us two *more* ideas to put together: the non-alignment of sexual identity with sexual attraction, and the heavy cultural endorsement of male sexual identity over against female. This means that men, *alienated* from women through cosmic loneliness, and seeing themselves as the more *emphasized* sex, interpret their alienation as a challenge to *dominate* women. The primordial alienation goes into the cultural mould of the master-slave paradigm. *Control* is the name of the game. And if we ask how the theologian interpreters of the Genesis text achieved the unanimous corporate oversight of seeing *loss of control* as the primary consequence of the

Fall where the text is saying that *awkwardness between the sexes* is the primary consequence, we surely have our answer: the text is being read with the eyes of the patriarchal mentality, for which man is the centre, woman the hazard, and control the name of the game.

Now the game is up, the patriarchal age is everywhere in crisis and indeed threatening us with extinction, and there is beginning the woman's quest for *her* identity, a quest of comparable magnitude with the male quest that has shaped three millennia. As I have mentioned, Karl Jaspers saw an 'axial shift' occurring around the sixth century B.C.—coincident with the tragedy of Oedipus Rex and the birth of the patriarchal age—and he described the present age as a second axial shift. He said, 'During this century it has been slowly dawning on us that scores of centuries are coming to a close.'

And in the middle of all this, we have the Catholic Church, which, institutionally, is the most patriarchal body there is. Its *idea* of sexuality, shaped by generations of male celibates and prescribed by a male celibate magisterium, is very much that of the patriarchal age, its implicit theme, 'Men, control yourselves (and control the women too).' Hence, I am sure, its failure to touch people today, even people of the best will in the world.

But I must leave you with a paradox. This same Church owes its existence and its meaning to an experience two thousand years ago, in which a small body of women and men knew the ending of cosmic loneliness, the liberation of the human psyche in Christ from all its barriers internal and external. If there is any community in the world that *ought* to understand that people don't like sex because they don't know God, that community is the Catholic Church. And that the patriarchal model *is* breaking down in the Church is suggested by the way a priest—Andrew Greeley—can say in a principal Catholic weekly that the pronouncements of the recent Roman Synod come from celibate men and evidence their dislike of sex and of women.

So there's my wide-angle vision, splayed out in all its paradoxical unmanageableness! The Church *is* committed to a strict and exacting sexual ethic, the reason for which is the high price that must be paid for sexual fulfilment. But people don't believe that that *is* the Church's reason. And, by and large, they are right!

Recapitulating these ideas on sex

Here, in bare outline, are the steps. The incest tabu, which holds together primitive society, sacralizes what it forbids: namely a sexual union that harmonizes passion with friendship (kinship). Through its solemn administering, the young person is brought, through the acknowledgement of family and tribe, into the appropriation of manhood or womanhood. The coming of genital experience is not, as in our society, an extraordinary accident to be privately negotiated as best one may. But this comfortable taking-on of sexual identity is only possible because of the very weak self-awareness that characterizes this stage in human history. Sexual identity, be it noted, is that final version of who one is which comes at age four or five. The primitive is not far removed from the animal condition in which *nature* tells him/her who he/she is. But with growing self-awareness, the human knows more and more fatefully that nature cannot do this job. To know my meaning as a man, or as a woman, I have to look *inward*. The tragedy *Oedipus Rex* marks the break from the old tabu-controlled sexual identity to the search of self-aware man for his identity.

I say 'man' here advisedly: because so massive, so Sisyphean, is the labour of this search that for its first three millennia western civilization has only managed half of it, and that none too well. And why all the fuss? Because my sexual being is the first big revelation to me of my *natural* being, of my being a product of nature: and *this* provokes in me the realization that that which tells me *what* I am cannot tell me *who* I am. And this condition, of seeking from my environment to know who I am and hearing only silence, is the most radical description of *loneliness* that there can be. Thus sexual identity does not find its meaning through the opposite sex, because it is a loneliness that questions the stars. That is why men have put their domestic life at risk by hitching their wagons to stars, and why women now are at last beginning to do the same. What we have

76

before us is a massive negotiation of a deep and ill-understood loneliness, a cosmic loneliness, a loneliness out of which we cannot lift each other. *And we have met it before.* It is the ineluctable inner loneliness that only an intimate experience of the creator can end for us.

Through the exploration of human sexuality, we have learned the *structure* of this loneliness: it is caused by the silence of nature in face of the self-questioning of nature's 'clearest-selved spark'. And when we realize that this same failure in dialogue occurs also in relation to our other two great natural involvements—our dependence on planetary resources and our mortality—we have a total picture of the human being: as the cosmic orphan whom desperation will drive to every wickedness and who will find fulfillment only in friendship with his/her joyful creative origin.

PART TWO

Ending The Inner Loneliness

Introducing Part Two

The theme of this book is an inner loneliness that only God can dispel. We have considered this loneliness, not only as a personal experience of loneliness, but as inscribed in human existence and showing itself with special acuity in the areas where we know ourselves as sexual beings, as hungry beings, and as mortal beings. We have seen, in other words, that the inner loneliness is the cosmic loneliness, a sense of cosmic orphanhood.

The mortal dimension we have hardly touched so far. Yet it is where we most acutely and fatefully experience this loneliness. Dying is the loneliest thing we shall ever do. And so, if God is to be experienced as dispelling our loneliness, this must happen *in our dying* if it is to happen, definitively, at all.

Yet there is a seemingly insuperable obstacle to such a divine communication. For death, the full realization of our loneliness, is out of our reach. We do not know anyone who has died. We have no experience of death *as* the crisis of our lonely yet desirous and hopeful existence. How then can God appear to us in death, now, and thus ground, now, an irrefragable faith in his friendship?

The purpose of this second part is to argue that precisely this prodigy of divine communication has occurred: that it was experienced by the disciples of Jesus, communicated by them, in the power of the Holy Spirit, to the Church, as the inner law of the Christian's growth.

Self-love without the split: Jesus

Jesus is the beginning of a new humanity, human being without the split in self-love between desire and control. Paul, in fact, calls Jesus the second Adam, and this has been one of his titles ever since.

It has been believed of him since the beginning that he was 'like us in all things but sin'. Now according to our analysis, the original, generic sin, whence all sins flow, is a radical distrust of our Creator, resulting, immediately and primarily, in a discomfort with our sexuality, an anxiety over our survival, and a dread of death. It follows, then, that human being free of sin would be totally trusting in God and consequently at ease with his/her sexuality, unanxious over survival, and without the dread of death as we experience that dread. And this is, in bare outline, the portrait of Jesus as we find it in the Gospels.

Let's spell this out. What we shall be doing is to put into words the great triangle that holds our picture together. We can start at the top. The unsplit self has an unsplit God. His God-image is whole. There is no trace of 'the God of desire as opposed to, and so opposed by, the God of control'. The God of desire fills the whole soul with his/her presence. The *will* of this God (what *we* think of as the control *side* of God) is totally obeyed out of desire. 'My food is to do the will of him who sent me.' 'My food', not 'my duty'.

Nearly all students of religion, Christian and non-Christian, agree that there is something about the religious experience of Jesus that is unique: an intimacy with God, a familiarity, not found in any other religious teacher. One of the strongest memories about Jesus is that he addressed God as 'Abba!' which is the Aramaic diminutive of 'Father'—what we could call 'Dad'. This is something unique in the history of religious experience. Now this familiarity with the ultimate mystery is what we would expect to find in a person not turned in from life by the split and projecting a split God. In the prayer and preaching, as in the behaviour of Jesus, we glimpse what the unsplit God is like. Instead of a God who is said to love us but threatens us with punishment—the normal God of religion—we have a God who wholly and only desires the fulfillment of our desire. Jesus is the person for whom the God of desire is absolutely to be trusted, can be totally invested in, is not hedged by 'the God of being on the safe side', the God of control.

As a result, the God of Jesus is significantly more connected with human flourishing, with children, with family, with community, than is the split God of religion. The God of Jesus promotes human flourishing and is evidenced by human flourishing. That is his/her only interest, because there is no 'other side' to this God. The central and organizing symbol of Jesus' teaching is 'the Kingdom of God', 'the Reign of God'. What such a phrase means to the split mind is 'Where all are doing what God (of control) tells them'. To the unsplit mind it means 'Where God is being allowed at last to give all human flourishing, where the sun is at last able to break through the clouds'.

Now just as God-forlornness results in the split with all its anxieties, so the whole God-awareness, the whole God-image, shows itself in a fundamental freedom from these anxieties. We can trace this freedom both in the life and in the teaching of Jesus. First, there is a huge freedom from the anxiety over survival. None of the normal concerns over livelihood hold him back, it seems, from a singleminded pursuit of his mission. One's image of Jesus is of a man on the move, not of a householder. Second, he appears to be comfortable with his sexuality in a way that sharply distinguishes him from the conventional image of the holy man of his time. In that very patriarchal society, the holy man kept himself aloof from women. Jesus, apparently, openly enjoyed the company of women and treated them as equals—which men have still not learned to do. This was remarked on, and gave offence. One's image of Jesus is of a man with women around him on an equal footing with men. All this stems from his freedom from 'shame'. Third, he moves towards his death as to a destiny. He does not look on death in the 'normal' way—as 'something that will happen but we don't think about it'. That is, he has an unrepressed attitude to death, as to life, and as to sexuality.

Reverting to our picture, consider the upper, 'guilt' split, which results from the split within self-love. This split (the guilt one) severely restricts the categories of people we are comfortable with. There are all sorts of people—like the winos who more and more accost one—whom we hurry past. One of the things emphasized about Jesus is his frequent dining with disreputable people—tax-collectors and prostitutes, for instance. Like his ease with women, this gave scandal to decent religious folk.

Next we consider the teaching. Its fullest statement is the 'Sermon on the Mount' or 'Great Sermon' in Matthew. The Sermon is almost certainly a collection of sayings pronounced on different occasions. And yet it has an extraordinary psychological unity. It is the teaching of a man freed by God from the basic anxieties and holding out this freedom to anyone who will open himself to God. The Eight Beatitudes are really eight different ways of saying, 'Normal, anxious people would say, "Happy the man or woman who has managed to allay to some extent the basic anxieties"; but I am saying, "Happy the man or woman whom *God* is *freeing* from these anxieties." ' The 'allayers' have put as big a distance as possible between themselves and poverty, sorrow, tragedy, loss. But once God is loose to promote human flourishing in his/her way, the more fortunate is the one who is closest to these things. And for Jesus, God *is* loose, hence the paradoxical beatitudes. It's not that God wants us poor, broken or sad. It's simply that in these conditions we are more likely to let him make us rich, whole and happy.

How essential to the teaching of Jesus is the new presence of God to the unsplit self, is brought out by considering the saying about the rich man and the camel going through the needle's eye. The disciples, who were *not* rich, asked, 'Then who can be saved?' In other words, they heard him saying, 'Unless you are un-hung-up from what every human being is hung-up on, you cannot be saved.' He was describing a work of detaching that only God can do, and that is the ecstatic consequence of being touched by God. And so his reply is, 'With humans this is impossible but not with God. All things are possible to God.' Only he who can do all things can detach me from sexual shame, the love-dread of death, and anxiety about food and drink, that is money—which, by a revealing slang, we call 'bread'.

The stringent, impossible demands in the Sermon are expressions not of strictness but of a phenomenal freedom. If you will let the real God come into your life, you will be free of the anxiety that makes it impossible to forgive injuries, to lend on demand, to 'turn the other cheek', and to look at an attractive person without lust. Once we remember that lust comes from the anxious condition called shame, we see that the God-given freedom from shame will result in a freedom from lust—that is to say, that compulsive way of looking at an attractive person that makes any open relationship impossible.

The whole sermon makes sense when you presuppose a new accessibility of the God of desire and life—and only then. The whole God-image makes all the difference. It makes the impossible possible—and immensely desirable. Once you're on course with this God, you will want to throw out anything that is going to stop you from reaching his Kingdom. The brutal hyperboles about plucking out the eye, cutting off the hand or foot, that confuse you, become understandable in this context—and in no other. Jesus' teaching is full of wild exaggerations. For Jesus is a wild man. He is unrestricted by our human fears. Finally, the Parables of Jesus are all ways of saying, 'There is the huge, impossible dream. And God will make it happen if you will let him/her.'

Entering the night of desire

Jesus formed a core group of disciples, men and women whom he invited into a closer relationship. These people picked up what a contemporary theologian has called the 'contagion' of Jesus.

What is this contagion? Here is my version of it, using the anthropology I have already worked out. The 'split self'—that is, the 'normal' self acquired from and transmitted to the culture—has a God of desire shadowed by a God of control, a God who is in human flourishing and a God who instills a certain distrust of happiness. Now imagine coming under the influence of one who knows nothing of this dark, untrustworthy God, whose God is 'Abba'—and not through a Pollyanna innocence but through a direction of his whole desire, the whole passion by which humans live, to the mystery that makes life one and whole. To understand the effect of this influence, we must recall that our *radical* belief is in the God of desire; desire *is* our experience of God moving us to more life. This radical conviction is fatally weakened, however, by 'the split', the failure of desire in a person to be wholly trusted. The effect on us of a person free of the split would be that the God of desire would for the first time be wholly believable, unshadowed by the God of control. Our desire, our trust in life, would *show* God to us. We experience this dynamic when we come into the company of an exceptionally strong and free person, and feel freer ourselves, no longer imposed upon by the bureaucrats who but yesterday intimidated us. All of us today have a great need to be freed from this intimidation.

What I have sketched so far is the first stage of the three-stage process through which the disciples of Jesus were led. I call it the 'intensification' stage. What happens here is that the part of the person that wants to *live*, the 'desire' or fulfillment-seeking part, is *intensified*, emboldened, enabled to throw off the paralysing fears engendered by the 'control' side. It is the 'falling-in-love' stage. We see it in anyone who finds a new purpose and meaning in life. Young people who became Marxists when I was young—and we were still innocent about the other side of Marxism—characterize this stage of spiritual development. There was a lyrical quality about their experience. What characterizes this stage is that what yesterday was 'something I'd *like* to do' today becomes 'something I *can* do'.

To understand the next stage, we have to ask: how does a person under this Jesus-influence stand in respect of the threefold primal anxiety with 'sex, food and death'? The *source* of this anxiety has not been removed. Only, the anxiety has been temporarily robbed of its power to confuse the person's sense of life and God. The anxiety has been suspended, not removed.

And, of course, the reason is that what may be called the person's dialogue with death is still, even in this ecstatically converted condition, the inconclusive affair it ever was, the affair whose only conclusion *is* death. The disciple of Jesus, even given the unique contagion of Jesus, is not and cannot be lifted out of our cosmic loneliness. On the contrary, he or she is, with special force, exposed to it. And here, we may begin to sense, lies the solution to that central problem of divine communication to which this second part is addressed. We may suspect, I mean, that the soul that Jesus has awakened to all that there is in our life is 'pointed', in a unique way, towards the crisis of death.

To make sense of this difficult notion, we must explore in greater depth the relationship between desire and death.

The process of transformation

A philosopher friend said to me recently that, desire or aspiration and death being the two big human facts, it is odd that no philosophy connects them. It is perhaps not so odd, for desire is now, hope is now, death future. More than that, death is the *end* of desire. It means no more desiring. It ends the whole vital climate in which desire thrives. So why should we connect desire with death except thus negatively?

But here we come up against the strangest part of all. Desire—we keep reiterating and know full well—is unlimited. We are never satisfied. It is for this reason that we project hopefully some quite other type of relationship in which desire would be satisfied. And death does appear to us in part—and this is the deeper part—not as simple extinction but as a severing of all our ties with this familiar human world, in other words, as the falling-away of limits. Now *this* idea of death, far from seeing in death the wholly unwelcome and to-be-indefinitely-postponed spoiler of the fun, suggests in death something congenial to desire: desire is without limits, and death is the falling-away of limits.

The statement that death may be congenial to desire wants very careful explaining. It is congenial only to that element in desire which chafes at limit. And we are never aware of this element by itself. We are only aware of it as the vague hope that somehow some other circumstance will bring the total fulfilment that is not possible in *these* circumstances. Of course 'some other circumstance' *means* 'another set of limits', but this fact is obscured, the indirectly envisaged 'other circumstances' doing duty for the desired world *without* limits. We do not appropriate our desire for the limitless, except in what Abbot Chapman calls the 'idiotic state' of contemplative prayer. It is only there that we aware, implicitly, of a 'loss of everything' that would be congenial to desire.

This affinity, therefore, between desire and death is never really put to the test in our experience. And in fact we do not know anyone who has died, for whom desire has been brought to this crisis of possible growth or liberation. Nor, of course, have *we* been through this crisis.

Now I suggest that the *image* of death as crisis accounts for the realization that we have to 'die', many times in our lives, if we are to grow spiritually; and that our not having experienced actual death gives to this process its non-definitive and having-to-be-repeated quality. We know that we must die often because we have not died once.

In other terms, our primordial connecting of desire with death is the source of our conviction that desire deepens through successive deaths, while the source itself, the connection itself, is, it seems, never experienced by us. If it were, if there were an experience of desire coming into its definitive crisis in death, that experience would be the unique experience of desire at its threshhold, of which *all* images of transformation, all rites of passage, the universal human image of death as a setting-sail, would be the reflections. I make this claim for the disciple of Jesus and for the faith they have given to us.

If there is, in desire, something for which death could be called congenial, that something is due to the limitless nature of desire. If, therefore, for some reason, the limitlessness of desire is experienced with a special intensity, then desire will be especially 'readied' for death. The 'great lover', for instance, whom joy has challenged to hope altogether beyond the normal limits, is brushing close to death, as all the creators of epic tragedy have inescapably understood.

Now the disciples of Jesus were in this condition to a unique degree. For they had caught the contagion of a person free from sin: free, that is, from that cosmic loneliness which is *the* brake on hope, on that central movement of desire which yearns for an infinite relationship.

This uniquely liberated desire was focused, was crystallized, in Jesus, who had awakened it. In a sense it was *more* crystallized in him than it was present in them. Or rather, their experience of it was fullest in this crystallization in him. For their desire was altogether beyond the scope of ordinary desire, and so it sought perforce a 'place to be', and he was that place. They could not take full responsibility for the way their hearts were moving. We see this phenomenon with all charismatic figures, who have to 'carry' in themselves much of what they are releasing in their followers. Simply to deplore the latter's immaturity in this transaction is to miss the point.

Thus it was the liberated infinity of desire in them, it was this precisely, that found in Jesus its place of rest, its place to be. And thus, if *their* desire was to come into the crisis of death, it was precisely *in his death* that this would happen. Far more critical than any 'death' that could come upon our ambition is the death that came upon *their* desire when *Jesus*, its focus, its centre, its meaning, was killed.

Is it not this special type of experience, of the hopes of a people crystallized in a charismatic figure who is put to death, that grounds the whole idea of redemptive sacrifice? Is it not, I mean, our *spiritual desire* that the victim carries in him or herself, that we see as mysteriously released with his blood? It may be that a theology of desire can join into one the two great ideas of Christ's death, as sacrifice and as transformation. The innocence of the victim, his sinlessness, is his beauty to us which draws out our desire and thus exposes it, in his death, to our death, the death that locks into our desire.

In their experience, then, of Jesus taken from them and put to death, they underwent *that* loosening of desire from its context that we call 'this world' which we *shall* undergo when we come to die. No other people have had this experience of 'dying while yet alive'. And all who have had an *analogous* experience of dying, metaphorically, while yet alive, have had an experience of which the disciples' experience is the 'prime analogate'.

His death was their death. It put them 'on the other side'. It projected their desire beyond time and space to where alone desire can be satisfied. It brought desire and death into the same reference-frame. They knew what the dead know. Death was no longer the shadow that broods over the only life we know. It had been gone through. There is in this experience a radical spaciousness of the soul, a totally new capacity to perceive. The mystics have a taste of it, in the dark night of the soul.

But now comes the most important question of all. Is this new capacity the condition of total fulfilment, of the ultimate bliss, of the final freedom? On the contrary, it carries a *need* that is as broad as the soul itself now is. Death as such does not introduce into the blissful presence: it only readies the soul for it, and the readying is a total emptying, a desolation. No real theism is compatible with a concept of death as simple breakthrough. Finite and infinite do not unite in that way.

So, once death has brought about the infinite emptiness, the latter needs to be filled by him who alone can fill it. This is the risenness of Jesus: his filling of the void that is 'on the other side', that *is* 'the other side'. This is the doxa, the divinity, the Spirit-giving of Jesus: his filling of the void that only God fills. Of this risenness, the empty tomb is a sort of strange aftermath.

He shines on the dead, who alone have eyes for him. He harrows hell, which alone is deep enough for him. He fills our emptiness, which is infinite and knows him who alone can fill it. He is Alpha and Omega, was dead (bringing us to death) and lives (bringing us to life), and holds the keys of death and hell.

This is risenness from the dead. The sight of him *raises* the dead, raises the seer from the ranks of the dead into which he has been introduced by the awesome Passion. It was impossible for him to be seen without the seer's being thus raised. And who are the dead? They are the to us unimaginable *subject* of the emptiness, the shadowy people of the emptiness, the people who are empty of all that fills us, the empty-handed. The pagan Hades, the Jewish Sheol, express this shadowiness of the dead when *compared* with us the living—obviously a distortion but a very human one. He who for us *fills* the emptiness, he who for us is *life* in the emptiness, who makes the emptiness vibrate with God, cannot be where we think of the dead as being.

The condition of the disciple, of being dead, is found in the pure state in the Good Friday interim. With the Easter experience, however, it remains as that which is filled, as the abiding and always re-entered prerequisite of the filling, as the foundational helplessness of the en-Spirited being, as the helplessness into which we must ever sink back, in a crisis of spiritual challenge, to be lifted up with Christ in the Spirit. The emptiness of which I am speaking is precisely that powerlessness in which Paul continually speaks— 'When I am weak, then I am strong.' It is the state of death, of disconnection, of losing all hold on things. The whole Pauline doctrine of weakness as the seat of the Power is located here. It appeals, ultimately, to that never-to-be-forgotten moment when Jesus was taken away from them for a fate that could not be in doubt. It appeals to that primordial collapse of our hold on life.

We are at the heart of what may be called the 'clean sweep thinking' of Paul. For Paul, *everything* is swept away, the past annihilated, 'sin destroyed in the flesh', the decree against us nailed to the cross and wiped out, and so *all* is new, God is all in all: the total emptiness admits the infinite in power: the experienced disconnection of death is transformed by the encounter with the one who wakes the dead. All Paul's soteriology, the sense that everything pours away on the gibbet of the new man, is in this great rhythm of emptying and filling, emptying of all, filling with 'glory'. For what is 'glory' but life in limitless abundance? How easily our stultified modern imagination sticks at the visual connotation of 'glory'!

The Pauline rhythm appears in the literary parallelism such as 'died for our sins, raised again for our justification'. It is far more than literary or rhetorical: its balance is not aesthetic. It is not a case of 'two sides of the same coin'. What is referred to is the massive *sequence* of emptying ('died for our sins', the taking-away movement) and filling ('rose again for our justification'). The statement that Christ 'died to sin' is a compact, a compendious statement, collapsing into one the death of Jesus and its immediate emptying effect. He 'dies us to sin, to the old world'.

The Pauline statement that 'the world is crucified to me and I to the world' is another way of referring to the total disconnection-with-all that the Jesus-crucifixion effects for the disciple. The mystical teacher *enjoins* 'detachment' from the world. Paul, in the power of the Spirit, *announces* 'crucifixion' of our relationship with it, doing to our relationship with the world what our death *will* do to it and what only Jesus' death, now, *can* do to it. Paul's doctrine of 'death to self' can now be better understood. Normally we take 'self' to mean selfishness, and 'death' as negative, the destroying, the ending of selfishness. But 'death to self' refers to the original disciple-experience, in which death (the real death we *shall* die) comes to the *desiring* self as the latter's crisis of transformation.

His death brought them to 'the other side'. But it isn't that, once you are on the other side, you necessarily 'see what's there'—Jesus in glory. The other side *as such* is empty, formless, helpless. There has to be the quickening of the dead soul by the living Jesus, by the 'life-giving Spirit' that, on one occasion, Jesus is said to have *become*. The preparation for this enlivening is not the effecting of it.

In my last book I called the Golgotha experience of the disciples 'the death of God'. What I was trying to express by this phrase was the end of our hold on God, on the goal of desire: an end that has to happen if our infinite desire is ever to be consummated. Gone is the old opposition between a *theologia crucis* and a *theologia gloriae*. Once the Golgotha experience of the disciple is seen as creating that total emptiness in which alone the glory can appear, the opposition loses all meaning.

How the new life, whose arising in the disciples of Jesus this book has studied, can pass into the convert to Christ, the early pagans for instance, needs to be considered; though I have no difficulty in seeing how *contagious* must have been the new life which God was manifestly bringing out of their death for the first heralds. And it is obviously significant that the convert had to *die* into the new life, in baptism. Would that our image of baptism could recover its original vitality and shed that notion of tokenism that sacraments perhaps inevitably acquire in the impoverished climate of the now played-out Enlightenment in which we still have to live.

Jesus says, in John, that the dead will hear the voice of the Son of God. Only the dead *can* hear that voice in its own accent. But only those who have *begun* to hear it, and then lost it, can *be* dead.

Ignatius speaks of 'consolation without a cause'. It is perhaps his most penetrating description of the mystical, of that deep sense in us whose stirring can only be from God. The Golgotha experience of the disciple sweeps away all 'causes'—and we may use that word also in the sense of 'things worth working for'—so that there can come upon the soul that reality which is wholly and absolutely its own. 'Consolation without a cause' is 'life where there has been only death'.

In conclusion, I may dare to add a ninth beatitude. Blessed are the dead, for they shall be raised up to renew the earth. There is the danger that my heavy concentration on the psychology of the disciples will lead to a confinement of the resurrection to psychology, to the neglect of its dimension of earth-renewal. But those who through the unique Jesus sequence *knew death*, knew what only the dead know, touched our very constitution in existence, touched our cosmology. And knowing the glory of their Master in that foundation of the world, they knew that the world itself was transformed. Otto Ranke has said, 'We are born beyond psychology and we die beyond psychology.' At the centre of world history, a small group of otherwise undistinguished people were led out onto that awesome promontory which is 'beyond psychology' and, through the life that there met and filled them, changed the world.

Coda

Crucial to this account has been the notion of death as a falling-away of all ties. This concept is classically described by Rilke in the latter part of his first Duino Elegy.

Now this idea of death is by itself enormously depressing. It does not by itself connote a breaking-free. It only connotes freedom if desire is fired with a supernatural hope, which it only *can* be definitively by Jesus Christ's act of filling the infinite emptiness of death with the Holy Spirit of the all-originating.

Still, infinitely depressing though it is without this presence of Jesus, the notion of death as the falling-away of all ties and meaning is the prerequisite to any possibility of faith in that presence. This notion of death is one *not* of extinction, but of a carrying to infinity of the loneliness in us. The notion of death as extinction is not only incompatible—obviously—with the resurrection faith. More importantly, it is not that which the resurrection faith displaces. Rather it expresses such a state of inattention to the self as cannot even raise the question of faith. I cannot think of myself as not existing. Certainly I can think of a world in which I do not exist. Of course a logician would object here, 'You cannot think of *anything* as not existing. But the things about which you now think *will* cease to exist. So, then, will you.' I am not clear as to how to answer this, but I am pretty certain that the answer has to do with the great divide, adumbrated earlier in this book, between those who think self-awareness is the same as self-reflection and that the self therefore has to be summoned to awareness as does Iceland or the Titanic, and those who know that this is not so. Somehow, the inalienable quality of self-awareness stretches, to our mind, 'beyond the grave'. And those whose more *reflective* mind is faithful to this inalienable quality envisage themselves, however depressingly or vaguely, 'beyond the grave'.

It has been suggested to me that my notion of death as a

94

falling-away of all connections is the Jewish notion, in so far as there can be said to be one Jewish notion. It is of great help to me to hear this. There is something seriously wrong about the statement, frequently made by Christian scholars, that the Jewish Scriptures in the main have no idea of survival. Were this so, Jewish religiousness could not be that highly self-aware religiousness that we know it to be. And if it is true, as I have argued, that the resurrection faith addresses itself not primarily to a fear of extinction but to the gloomy survival of Sheol or Hades, then I would expect *that* faith to which Christ offers a wonderful opening-out to *have* a concept of survival, and not a hopeful one. The Jewish idea of Sheol is a true idea of the state after death without Christ, without the resurrection. We have lost this capacity to think of 'survival without fulfilment', because our Christian habit of mind packages together survival and fulfilment in face of a materialist culture that denies both. And of course Pascal's 'wager' works on the supposition that they are one. If there is no God, well, you won't be the loser by your pious moral existence, for there won't be any more you. This distorts and privatizes the Christian hope. The meaning of the traditional belief that Jesus saves us from hell is that, if there is no God and Jesus and Holy Spirit, we are all going to hell.

In short, there is a fatal confusion, in the Christian mind, between 'survival' and 'blissful survival'. It is the latter that our faith offers *in contradistinction to the former*. The hope of a blissful immortality arises not from death as foreseen and speculated about, or as 're-vealed' about, but from death as anticipated by the disciple of the Crucified and thus awakening to the taste of Christ in the Spirit of the eternal ground of being.

Easter 1981

Out of the dreaded end comes endless life:
those who have died live every place and time,
their blood still with them they renew the earth,
dissolve in love for life the grossest crime.

The flesh's silence to the spirit's question
their God has broken, bringing them to know
death in this world, and life that throbs outside
its prison present and predicted flow.

Even before this change has come to us
we know that we are infinite by the flesh:
thus enigmatic we remain until
we know the flesh by the infinite's caress.

All honour to one man who dying drew
the heart his way to life unbound in death:
in him we see ourselves live, dead, undying:
three worlds made one, feeling the Spirit's breath.

Bitter his labour in the middle world
where death must meet desire to set it free:
easeful his being now to lonely hearts
who cry with joy as intimately 'we'.

He says: I died and live and reign for you,
unlock heart's prison, death, and draw you on
changing your lonely dread to happy fear:
desire infinite—and not alone!
                    (Sebastian Moore)

The Riddle

The friend of God we had to kill,
he was too close to our desire:
the friend of God we had to lose:
his death would bring us to the fire.
                    (Sebastian Moore)

The soul's drama

I would meet you upon this honestly.
I that was near your heart was removed therefrom
To lose beauty in terror, terror in inquisition.

T. S. Eliot
'Gerontion'

There is a five-act drama of the human soul. Act 1 is limitless desire. Act 2 is the advent of fear, the fear that arises, in the nature of the case, from the sense of the unforeseeable character of our future as we live out our desirous, outgoing existence. Now the event that above all embodies this entry on an unforeseeable future is death. With death we enter the unknown, an existence where we have no control, only the poverty of sheer desire, sheer need, the unavoidable passivity to an all-transcending mystery. And so it is on death as this entry into the unknown that the fear of Act 2 focuses.

Thus the fear of death, in its first incidence in the drama of the soul, is the fear of the unknown. Its context is the adventure of the soul. But fear is a tricky customer. It has quicksilver mobility. And once we *succumb* to the natural fear that constitutes the second moment in our story, it quickly transforms the *reason* for fearing death *from* its being the encounter with the unknown *to* its being, quite simply, 'the end of me'. The fear of death loses its original context (Act 2) and becomes a gripping finality. Thus it becomes a new, and quite different, and indeed an opposite, terror. As against the terror of entering a new, unknown existence, the terror of no more existence of any kind.

This latter is the 'terror of death' as Becker understands it. I wonder, more and more, whether 'terror' is the right word for the prospect of 'no more me'. Would it not be truer to say that this thought is not terrifying but infinitely *depressing*; and that it is as depressing, and not as terrifying, that it is and must be *repressed?*

Act 3, then, features the translation of the fear of death out of its pristine context of encounter with the unknown to where it broods over us without hope—'not here the darkness, In this twittering world' ('Burnt Norton' from *Four Quartets*)—and really loses the name and vigour of fear and becomes a *depressive thought* that would sap all motivation.

From which Act 4 of necessity follows. In the interests of self-preservation, the psyche represses the thought of death. Act 5 is our life built on these ruins. But this self-preservation is on terms pathetically more limited than those offered in the totality of our human drama.

And conversely, nor is our plight to be remedied by the 'de-repression' of Act 3's dread of death, by learning to live with an infinitely depressing (and invalid) thought. The Heideggerian heroism?

Our plight is remedied only by getting past Act 3 to Act 2: by restoring our dread from the doldrums of a depressing nihilism to 'the dark cold, the empty desolation, the vast waters' of the night of God ('East Coker' from *Four Quartets*). This is what happens in the Jesus event. The disciples are thrown into a uniquely potent Act 2 out of a totally de-repressed Act 1. Jesus, *the* man of desire, awakes the deepest and most total hope in the hearts and minds of his followers. And the dread that *this* reactively awakens finds a death to focus on that will represent to the soul absolutely *all* that is dreaded by reason of the mystery that allures and daunts it: the abysmal death of Jesus. In that event, and in that event alone, the death that awaits us all and that sends harbingers of itself into our daily life is wholly set in its context, its true, full context, where it has us dangling from the hand of the unknown. It is Jesus experienced where God has the next move. It is Jesus *as* the next move.

The faith that is born of this encounter—and for Lonergan, faith is 'the knowledge generated by religious love'—is, for the first time, life not *beyond* death (that was known already), not life *after* death (so was that), not life *against* death (that is a desperate claim), not life *over* death, but life *out of* death. The power of death—or rather the power of fear to transfer death from its true meaning to a hopeless finality—has been forever annulled.

Freud once said, to a patient, words to this effect: I cannot make you happy, but I can restore you to the unhappiness that is proper to the human condition (out of your purely private, neurotic misery). Jesus says something like this: I will not make you happy on your terms, but I can restore your dread of death from the condition in which you must forget it to the condition where you have nothing to hold you but the everlasting arms, in whose embrace is eternal happiness.

The drama, and its divine redirection, is worked out primarily in the area of our mortality. But it must work out similarly in the other two crisis areas, of sexuality and of survival—or, to be more concrete, of sex and money. Corresponding to the declension from the fear of death as embrace of the unknown to the dread of death as a final horizon would be a declension from sexual shame as awe at something mysterious to sexual experience as 'all there is', as a horizon to be explored through its 360 degrees but never crossed. And do not many people today accord a *kind* of finality to 'sex' that they accord to death? And is there not an 'Act 4' for sexuality? Is it perhaps 'sex is all there is' that is being repressed in what is called sexual repression? Is 'sex' repressed, as 'death' is, because it is boring, because it is failing to be exciting as God means it to be? Similarly, our anxiety over survival has lost the sense of awe and mystery (to which the Sermon on the Mount seeks to restore it) and *therefore* is repressed.

In Acts 3 and 4 sex as a purely animal function is boring and has to be repressed.

Death as a purely animal event is depressing and has to be repressed.

Survival as a purely animal necessity is unexciting and has to be repressed.

A Christian sexual ethic, if we ever have one, will be an ethic that restores sexuality to its original context, the life of this peculiar being whose desiring is the life of infinite spirit, whose body is the language of this life.

PART THREE

The Infinite Unloneliness

The mystical dogmatized—the Trinity

I have sought to get at the idea of God through the fact of inner loneliness. The reason why nothing and no one in this world can relieve my inner loneliness is that all share it, all partake of it. When I speak of this loneliness, I am speaking of 'everything that there is *becoming* "world" for me by reason of the very nature of my self-awareness'. The very ancient idea of the human being as the microcosm of the universe is only a naive, extroverted version of our primary self-awareness, which is our world-ing of all things. It is this sense of 'it all coming to a head in me' that makes of me a lonely 'head'.

Now there is something strange about this account. For do we not more readily think of the ultimate spiritual loneliness as *a*cosmic, feeling myself a *stranger* to this world, standing over against the world?

There is no contradiction here. The deepest reason for the strangeness to me of another, even of an intimate, is that the other is *as lonely as I am*. The more intimate two persons become, the more there opens up this deeper dimension of existence in which all share a common loneliness. Personal intimacy exposes the human loneliness. Existence is lonely, and the more that people, through intimacy, exist, the more lonely they become.

I think, then, that it is misleading to say that it is an infinite narcissism that requires 'one who is the idea of me being', for this implies in me a loneliness *apart* from the world; whereas the clamour of the God-desire results in the *pressure*, on me, *of* the whole world. Not only the world's failure to relieve my loneliness but, more radically, the reason for this failure—namely its being part of the one indivisible lonely situation—is the thing that makes me lonely. And thus it is *all being* that clamours, in me, not to be lonely. It is the hills and the trees, the sunsets and the villages, that clamour not to be all that there is about themselves. In Heideggerian terms, it is as the shepherd of being that the human is lonely. It is by being part of my loneliness that the world is incapable of relieving it.

It is this loneliness that arises, of necessity, out of the heart of experiencing that the world is, that yearns for a mysterious communion that would relieve it. In search of this mysterious other, I do not look away from, or outside, the world, but beyond it. And this really means that in me the world looks beyond itself. I represent and experience the loneliness of all being. In me the galaxies hunger for God. In me all the world craves his companionship.

And what is the loneliness of being? It is the loneliness of simply being, without reason, without meaning, the loneliness of facticity. And what can relieve this loneliness? Only a 'who' can relieve *any* loneliness, so we must rephrase the question accordingly. The reliever of this loneliness must be absolutely *interior* to being. And he/she must be the meaning. Perhaps we may say that being—always remembering that we are thinking of an experience—*in search of* meaning conceives the *idea* of being. I think of 'my idea'. And indeed we see people's lives as a kind of dialogue with 'the idea of myself'. But the *idea* of being, the idea of all-in-me-and-me-in-all, is only a wishful projection, a whistling in the dark, unless this idea *is*, subsists, infinitely and unimaginably deserves the description 'who'. It is such a 'who', such a subsisting thought of all that there is or could be, that the lonely shepherd of being craves for there to be. And so we arrive, through analysis of the heart's need, of the need of a heart made lonely by all finite being sharing its loneliness, at *ipsum esse subsistens*.

It is *being* that is lonely for its living idea, and not an isolated self. Take off the pressure of all that is and could be and, whatever you have, you do not have the human loneliness. And if we return to the literary models for this loneliness—the young suicide in James Baldwin's *Just Above My Head*, for instance—what we find there is precisely the seemingly impossible—only not impossible to faith—requirement that 'the whole *thing* be different'. The most unreasonable and therefore individual feature of the demand is precisely the universality of its scope. Eliot hits the same mark in *The Family Reunion*.

Harry: But I though I might escape from one life to another,
And it may be all one life, with no escape. (*Part II, scene 2*)

*   *   *

Harry: I was like that in a way, so long as I could think
       Even of my own life as an isolated ruin,
       A casual bit of waste in an orderly universe.
       But it begins to seem just part of some huge disaster,
       Some monstrous mistake and aberration
       Of all men, of the world, which I cannot put in order.
       (*Part II, scene 1*)

                *   *   *

Harry: So you must believe
       That I suffer from delusions. It is not my conscience,
       Not my mind, that is diseased, but the world I have to
       live in. (*Part I, scene 1*)

What is meant by original sin consciousness is 'the whole, in loneliness', all being coming to a head in the person and stopping there. Eliot is giving us its pathology in the most important of his plays. Harry has unknowingly tried to escape from the enclosing whole of the world into which he is woven by all the ties of an unhappy family, that whole which spells his ultimate loneliness, by pushing (or dreaming of pushing) his wife off the deck. Through this attempt, he has made the enclosing whole 'active', claiming him, in the shape of the Eumenides. The whole will be—for him as for Nietzsche—a horror, the deepest loneliness ('the unexpected crash of the iron cataract') until the moment of grace when 'the awful eye' *above* the whole reveals itself. Then the Eumenides become 'the bright angels'.

Now comes a most important question. If there is *ipsum esse subsistens*, the living idea of all in me and me in all, if there is this absolute un-lonely-ing of being, then who am I? The crucial and all-transforming belief that there is this living idea of being says something about the self-awareness available to one who consciously is. What does it say? What or who is the 'self of this world' that, radically not lonely, corresponds with the living negation of loneliness at the heart of existence? What response does this heart of being call forth in being? What is the freedom that responds to this blissful ultimate reality, to bliss being the ultimate reality? Whose is this freedom?

Before we try to answer this question, we must be clear as to the implications of there *being* an answer, there being such a 'self'. First, it is not a self that a person could develop, like character or ego. It absolutely precedes all effort, and indeed can only become manifest with the cessation of effort. It is a self *into* which a person comes, and *in* which the person has always, unknowingly, been. And since it absolutely precedes all human effort and decision, it at least 'behaves' as God behaves. And so radically does it respond to the originating bliss, that it *is* response. It is God's response to himself. It is God *in* the world responding to God *beyond* the world.

There is a fascinating feature about the Arian controversy that generally escapes notice. What Arius was formally denying was not the divinity of Christ (though this denial was implied) but the divinity of who Christ was universally agreed to be. The controversy concerned not the Christ of memory and faith (except implicitly) but that mysterious reality *in the world*, in the cosmos, that responds, or *in* which the world responds, to the blissful origin. The biblical sapiential literature contains some beautiful meditations on this reality. And what Arius was saying *of this mysterious reality*—and not, except by implication, of the obviously and scandalously finite being Jesus of Nazareth—was that it could not be God. What Arius represents is a failure to relax all the way into a God who plays in this world. He represents a foreshortened theism in which the creature, in the last resort, is struggling towards God, not participating in God's play with himself. He does not enjoy the light of there being the living idea of being, the light that this sheds on the world, the self that this involves there being within the world, the self that is God responding to God (in that love which, in God's creative life, wholly replaces the role of interest, curiosity and attraction by the other, by the light and by the way paint behaves, in our creative operations. Augustine understood this in his *De Trinitate*. He saw the procession of the Spirit *within* the procession of the Word.)

The decision of the Church against Arius is momentous in its implications. It is that this reality commonly called 'word', this being of God in the world for the spiritual creature to discover himself in, *is* God, one in being with the all-originating reality. The momentous implication is that the manner of the spiritual creature's response to God, that will become fully explicit in Jesus Christ, is already sketched out as to its essential structure. It will consist not in any humanly originated effort, not in any attempt to stretch beyond itself to God, but in coming into a centre that *is* God in response to God, coming into a cycle of divine life. The most mature Pauline statement, in Ephesians, that God has made us to sit with Christ in the heavenly places and that therefore our whole religious and ethical life is the follow-through of this gratuitous divine insertion of us *in* divinity, is but the concrete implementation of this

106

basic rhythm. And while the christological realization of the rhythm is infinitely more excellent than the rhythm conceived in these more abstract terms, Christology must fall seriously short if this abstract foundation is ignored and the Word that is 'made flesh' is not regarded as being, previously to this, in the world.

It is, of course, easy to blur the absolute distinction between God and creation in our description of this God-responsive reality in the world. We can, I think, avoid this trap by insisting that what all this discourse is concerned with is not the *status* of the creature, which cannot in any sense be divine, but the *mode of access* of the creature to God; which mode of access is through coming into a divine centre which responds to the divine origin. Of this divine centre, some Catholic mystics have said, 'it is my true "I" ', and it got them into trouble, but they were never in any doubt that this centre, pre-eminently deserving to be called, by the mystic, 'my true "I" ' in so far as 'I' implies centre and this reality is *the* centre, was absolutely transcendent and not to be confused with the creature. The key to this mysticism is the doctrine of the Trinity, that the creature's response to God is a being taken up into a mysterious response of God to himself. God within the self is the self's true way to God beyond the self. All other ways of self-transcendence are touched with pride and doomed to fall short. Paradoxically, it is the recognition of the divinity of the self in this sense, of the divinity of my centre, that saves my movement beyond myself from being the subtle negation of my creaturehood that it otherwise is.

I am intrigued, therefore, by the suggestion that the doctrine of the Trinity is dogmatized mystical experience. This is surely correct. What it means is that the mystical tradition, which is the most responsive to the reality 'that all call God', has regularly found that it is *out of* a transcendent centre that the soul moves *to* the transcendent, and that this centre is 'of' the transcendent not as awakened in it in response to God as a challenging other (as my idea is born of me in response to a challenging object) but simply as of love with which the transcendent is identical.

The meaning of the Holy Spirit is that, God being all that there is in all that there is, only love, as opposed to interest in reality-as-other, can account for his self-expression in the world. In traditional trinitarian language, the Son is born as Word, of the love Spirit, that God is. The Father is distinguished from the Son only as begetting, not as love, *in* which he begets. The reason why love, in God, is one of the mysterious entities traditionally known as persons is that love in God does not *result* but *originates*. God does not respond with love, is not attracted, but originates love, is the origin of love. Love in God, then, is 'produced', and thus is 'substantial'. And all this because God is God, the absolutely original, the absolutely originating, an eternal process of self-affirming in self-love. God originates love out of himself, and in this love God affirms himself. The 'second procession' is not resultant on the first but is within the first.

In sum, the main implication of 'Christ is God' is that the centre out of which we move to the transcendent is itself transcendent. The belief that Christ is God is the belief that prayer is mystical, divine in origin and in goal.

From the divinity of the Word, of the transcendent centre of the creature, the divinity that was what Arius denied, to the identification, by that divinity, of Jesus, the essential progression is as follows. Finally, intentionally, we have to experience ourselves as centred in this transcendent centre. Now the process whereby we are brought to this centring has to embrace the tragic totality of our life; it cannot just be the 'moment' of prayer or selfless action. It has to come through the death in which all our life culminates. But *our* death remains obstinately future. Yet unless it is made present to us it cannot be, in life, in desire, our bringing in to the centre. The way this comes about is through a process in which Jesus stands revealed as doing in us what only God can do, and thus as God. Specifically, this man awakens our desire at a new depth, and thus perforce becomes its focus. Put to death, he brings our desire through that crisis of desire in which, precisely, the ego is transcended and a new transcendent centre of desire is acknowledged, accepted, centred in and lived. Thus the divinity of Jesus is essential to the existential centring of us in the transcendent Word or Son or 'world-self'.

St Paul's metaphor for this centring is in Ephesians (1:17–21; 2:6–9). It is commented by Watchman Nee in his short book, *Sit, Walk, Stand*, which is quite the most exciting thing on Paul that I have ever read.

Relax into the warm blood of the Lamb
into the self of God in the whole world:
Christ died for me to be this way, thus selved
in gentleness to everyone I meet.

God died for God, the blood the Holy Spirit,
God lives for God, the life the Holy Spirit:
this world and all it owns is lost until
released into the life-blood of the Lamb.

Jesus Christ my more than wisdom,
my dying, rather, into God:
how can I doubt to eat and drink him,
flesh and blood the soul's own food.
                    (Sebastian Moore)

Beata Trinitas

God is God. This massive tautology is the ground of all our thinking. It is necessary as a continual reminder of something of which, in the nature of the case, only a tautology can keep us mindful. It means: God has no definition. God is not this or that. God simply is God, himself/herself/itself, beyond definition, incomprehensible, his own reality. To say 'man is man' is uselessly tautological, for it has no function as a reminder that man cannot be defined, cannot be called this or that; for man can and must be called this or that. 'God is God', on the other hand, heads us continually off the inveterate temptation to make God comprehensible. God is beyond all our notions, all the categories in which we seek understanding.

Now the most radical of our categories of self-understanding, in other words of the understanding of conscious being, are knowing and loving. God, then, is beyond knowing and loving. But it would be better to say that God is *behind* knowing and loving, or that God is the *origin* of knowing and loving. If God is the origin of knowing and loving, then God *is* knowing and loving, and this is a more mysterious statement than appears, that God *is* knowledge and love. This statement, far from defining God as linguistically it appears to do, goes in the reverse direction, of making us wonder whether we know what knowing and loving are. This statement about the unknown, that it *is* knowing and love, backfires onto what we took to be the known, knowing and love.

Now to say that God is an original and incomprehensible reality behind, or originating, knowing and love, is to put up the question as to what 'behind' or 'originating' means. It is to ask for some idea of *how* knowing and loving may be understood as derivative from a reality beyond them or containing them or originating them. In other words, the originating or 'principal' character of this reality can only show itself *in the deriving*, from it, of knowing and loving.

110

As mysterious as a reality beyond knowing and love is the springing of knowing and love from that reality. This we have now to consider.

The first thing to realize is that the reason why knowing and love here derive from a mysterious reality beyond them is that that reality is God. For the reason why knowing and love are, for us, *not* derivative realities but original is that we are finite beings among finite beings that excite our curiosity, awaken our interest, offer themselves for closer inspection and study, and even call forth an all-sacrificing love; and we don't know *why* all this happens at all. The response generated in us by the unknown other is the original given of our existence. There just *is* loving and knowing. Without them our life would be without meaning. For us, knowing and loving are unquestionable absolutes. We cannot think of *them* as derivates.

And yet when we come to God we find that somehow we have to. The reason is that for God there is not that surprisingness, challengingness, intriguingness of the other which for us makes knowing and loving to be absolutes not to be derived from anything more radical. God is all in all, infinite, self-sufficient. God, then, does not look to knowing and love to connect him with the real. He *is* the real, he is reality. Because he *is* reality, knowing and love in him are in some strange position, have some strange role, that is consonant with this total self-sufficiency, this equation with all reality. Because God is God, knowing and love in God are strange, are the extension, or the extendedness, or the structure, of an all-originating mystery. They are not the structure of reality as pre-sented to God, as they are to us. They are the structure of God's reality, which *is* reality.

Can we say more, can we be more precise about this strange behaviour of love and knowing in God? Well, certainly we can, and must, say a great deal more than we have hitherto said about human knowing and loving.

An idea of human knowing that Aquinas took over from Augus-tine and others and found useful for building up his analogy for the Trinity is proving today to be surprisingly relevant. To know some-thing is to 'speak' it to oneself, to let something happen in one's mind, to let a process go forward. The vague hunch gives way to attention and inquiry, hypothesis and approximations pour out. The process is enormously variegated and complex, but its core is the 'inner speaking', the making explicit. With this very ancient model for what knowing is, some teasing problems can be solved.

In his brilliant book *Self-Deception*, Herbert Fingarette shows that the heart of self-deception is a nearly imperceptible refusal to 'let the word speak itself'. The unfortunate people in Hitler's Germany really did *not* know about the camps, as they themselves declared. They did not allow a diffused sense of evil and wrong to become, in them, the knowing act—for obvious reasons. And it has occurred to me that we may clear up the appalling conceptual confusion of the psychoanalytic 'conscious' and 'unconscious' mind, by calling these respectively the 'spoken' and the 'unspoken' mind.

Now the most mysterious part of this process is the question about all the factors involved in the 'decision' to 'let the word come' or not. We are, in fact, in the vast area of what is called the unconscious—the diffused misery of life in Hitler's nightmare Germany, the obscure promptings of genius and of sanctity, the movement of conversion and of creative response to therapy, the almost imperceptible dreams taken seriously, the mindbirths that 'make it' to the weal or woe of humankind. The robust Thomist axiom *nil amatum nisi precognitum* covers a minefield of complexities. Specifically, the brilliant, attention-drawing *formulation* of the genius not only releases the enthusiastic loving response, but, very hiddenly, owes its origins to that strange thing we call 'interest', which is itself a form of love. In place of the simplistic picture of being presented with an object which, once known, can be loved, we should speak of a mysterious intentionality in a person, a hunger for meaningful life, an eros, that obscurely dictates the explicitating of the rich reality *so that* it may fully deploy itself in love.

Now in the case of God, what may we speak of in place of this initial eros? It has no sense of incompleteness, of striving to come to birth. And so it does not initiate knowing, the speaking of the word, *in order to* complete itself as love. It is itself complete, an absolute abundance of love, *in* which, in absolute abundance, the word is spoken. God, the absolutely original beyond knowing and loving (which we can only conceive in terms of the attracting other) lovingly knows himself, lovingly speaks himself as all that there is.

The Holy spirit, then, is not love as *resultant* on what God knows in the Word. For a hint of what the Holy Spirit is, we have to go to the 'initial eros' in human knowing—to that area, in fact, about which we do use words like 'inspired', 'genius': we speak of 'the spirit' of a leader. In one fascinating text, Paul makes the connection explicit. The Holy Spirit knows the deep things of God, he says, *as* the spirit of a man—and it alone—knows the things that are in him.

The unimaginable difference is that whereas the spirit of a man or woman, instinct with all the reality around him or her, impels towards the speaking of many 'words' in order to come to a full relationship with the real, the Spirit of God is complete, total, infinite in scope, and in this infinity of joy the one Word is spoken.

It would appear, then, that the derivative, as opposed to the simply imposed, nature of knowing and love in God shows itself in a significantly different order *between* knowing and love. Instead of the highly complex dialectic between knowing and loving whereby the human being comes to fruition, each looks to the other *ex abundantia*, the infinite joy, the sheer spirit in him who is, finding a free, non-functional expression in the Word. For the *ratio* of the dialectic of knowing and love is that these are our indispensable tools for connecting with the real: simply given to us, they have to be used 'economically'. God who is all reality needs no tools; his knowing and loving do not have tool-status, and so they don't interconnect in our economic way. God is a total binge of joy, love, wisdom, intelligence.

Thus the Trinity is the way it is because God is God. Because God is the original mystery whence is all reality, knowing and loving which for us *reflect* reality *originate* for God. The divine 'processions' are these originatings, these arisings, out of the depths of the divine nature, of that knowing and loving which for us finite beings are ultimate and not derived realities.

Now to say that the Trinity is the way it is because God is God is to say that the Trinity *is* the divine nature. It is the failure to understand this that perforce creates a dichotomy between 'the divine nature' and 'the Trinity': since divinity as such is not understood to be, as above, originating of knowledge and love, or trinitarian, the divine nature and the Trinity fall conceptually apart. The Trinity thus comes to be thought of as a highly mysterious 'inner life of God', somehow behind the divine nature. The expression 'inner life of God' is, significantly, meaningless. And I use the term 'highly mysterious' ironically to indicate the type of mysteriousness that is generated when the Trinity, no longer seen as the mystery of the Godhead in its transcendence of knowing and loving, is left to the theologian's ingenuity. And in this loss of creative touch with the mystery, we lose touch even with the most mysterious thing about our own spiritual operations, which is the grounding eros, which gives the clue to the Holy Spirit. The Spirit then appears as a shadowy resultant on the first procession, and one of the problems is to see how this resultant can be seen as a procession at all. Not surprisingly, the Spirit emerges as the dullest part of the picture, whereas it is the vibrancy of the whole. The Spirit becomes mysterious in the sense of problematical, instead of being the infinite version of that which, even in the phenomenon of human creativity, is vastly and intriguingly mysterious. The 'mystery' of the Trinity comes to mean 'how there applies in God an oversimplified and lifeless model of knowing and loving'. There doesn't, of course.

Finally, though Eckhart is regularly interpreted as himself separating the Godhead from the Trinity—in his case to exalt the former over the latter—it may be that what he is really talking about, in his flowing of the Trinity *out of* the Godhead, is precisely that *derivation* of knowing and loving in the self-sufficient Infinite which manifests that being beyond, or behind, or origin of, knowing and loving, which is what it means for God to be God.

Reflections

1. When I feel attracted to a person, I feel loved, cherished, enlarged, by that person's *being*, whatever the person feels or does not feel. I hope that the person will come closer to his/her being as I am feeling it, and perhaps feel loved, cherished, enlarged, by *my* being. Which means that in love we are more interested in what we *are* for each other than in what we *do* for each other. The referent, the bottom line, of love is my given, not self-made, being, my body with its peculiarities, my character with its quirks, precisely the things I can take no credit for, this heavy, inescapable me. The referent of loving is God.

2. Love is, in its essence, mutual. Its outgoingness to the other who attracts me is, identically, my lovedness by the other's being, whether the other knows/wills this or not.

3. Jesus: in his ministry, the awakener and focus of the desire for God; in death, the bringer of the desire to the other side; beyond death, the consummation of the desire in the Holy Spirit of the eternal Father/Mother.

4. 'No one comes to the Father but by me.' Through me alone, you plunge through suffering into death, while still alive, and beyond death into the bliss that God is.

5. The unknown all-embracing one
   is known to love only
   for love is indivisible,
   excludes nothing and nobody.
   I cannot stir in this darkness
   but with my feeling for all.
   O that forgotten deeply lost
   feeling for all! (Sebastian Moore)

6. According to John Knowles, author of *A Separate Piece*, French has no word for lonely and no word for home. What will it make

of the root-concept of my theology: ineluctable inner loneliness, cosmic orphanhood or homelessness?

7. The important distinction to be made is not between love for a human being and love for God, but between love for only one human being and that love which, stirring towards God, extends to all human beings.

8. 'Old wine into new skins' makes sense, provided the 'old wine' is contemplative prayer tradition; not if it is an obsolete Catholic style, cosmetized to look contemporary.

9. Classical salvation doctrine has seen the drama of Jesus as played out in the sight of God. We have to see it as played out in the experience of the men and women it transformed and transforms in the presence of God. Jesus *was* their desire, being its awakener and focus: so his death was death for their desire, its plunge beyond this limiting world.

10. In the life, death and resurrection of Jesus, the mystical transcending of space and time is realized in the whole of our mortal existence.

11. The idea of me is what all call God. The self, the ratio of my being, is what all call God. *Ipsum esse subsistens*: the idea of me being, alive. The home of me is what all call God.

12. Death evades us. Absurdly we are kept alive in this time when all that we may hope for is on the other side. Indeed we are borne on now with only desire, our destination Jerusalem, where all that awaits us is the other side of death. Only let desire fix where it will: on him who will be killed there, whose blood we drink in hope.

13. What have I been talking about, unwittingly, when I said that desire and death had to meet? About everything. About everything that lies beyond our normal ego-consciousness, that all to which our insatiable desire extends, that all which is on the other side of death. I am talking about Prince Ring (and many other tales), in which the Prince, losing his hunting companions, sees a stag with a ring on one of its antlers and follows the stag and goes through various death-like adventures. The ring awakens and focuses desire (to be himself, Ring), as Jesus awakens and focuses the disciples' desire. The ring disappears, Jesus is killed, and desire is lost in the night of faith. In the night, life is transformed, Jesus is raised.

14. The death of a loved one is his/hers alone, not that of the bereaved. But the death of Jesus is not his alone but theirs too: for

116

the essential desire that everyone's life is, is in that case brought to recognition and focused in him. He *is* the desire by which all live. So his death is theirs: living they die, as their desire is plunged into the awful emptiness. And finds there new members. Finds there the Body of Christ.

15. The other side: the unconscious. 'God and the Unconscious'. Eliot talks of 'death's dream kingdom' and of 'death's other kingdom'. Jesus led them into death's other kingdom. About three years ago, I was comparing the resurrection encounters with dream experiences. Now I see that it is dream experiences that palely reflect the resurrection encounters, the experience in death's other kingdom.

16. It came to me this morning in prayer: another self, another centre, all care thrown away, gone all the heaviness of caring for myself, no need to any more.

17. If there is *ipsum esse subsistens*, the living idea of me and all, of all in me and me in all, then who am *I*? Who am I in whom all is? The green hugeness of Downside brings back this experience as it first gave it me. I am the response to this living idea of me-and-all, I am the divinity of all creation, its reflectiveness of the logos, the freedom of creation in the Son. I live now, not I, but Christ lives in me. The ultimate relationship is not *to* God but *in* God. It is trinitarian. *I* am trinitarian in my taken-over-ness. My true self *is* divine without pantheism. Christ has broken the ancient alternative: either a stern Islamic *to*-God monotheism, or break God into everything. God has broken out *himself* into everything. In Jesus, the reflection of *ipsum esse subsistens*, he has pervaded all that is. Making peace by the blood of his cross. For there has to be the cross: this envelope of flesh had to be broken open to 'the other side'.

These realities, of Trinity and incarnation, are frequently preached and written about, but there is seldom evidence, in this preaching and writing, of their appropriation, intellectual and aesthetic and moral. The excellent book by Pennington (*Centering Prayer*), whenever it touches base, does so by saying, 'by baptism we are brought into the life of the Trinity'. True. But what kind of an understanding of this truth can we have if we can only express it in terms of an inner life of the Godhead with which we connect only through a ceremony?

18. In me all the world craves his companionship.

117

19. God originates knowing and loving, in knowing himself out of love, out of the original joy of his being.

20. Self-awareness is sexual, so self-exposure has primary sexual connotations. Nudism is self-conscious, and would only not be so in an Edenic condition. The most intimate visible signature on a person's selfhood is his/her manifest sexuality. There is then an inalienable connection between sexual identity and the sense of dependence on that something more self than myself, unimaginably interior to the whole inescapable pursuit of life, that all call God. We cannot dissociate the way people hide their sex from the way they hide their fear and desire of God. And we only hide with passion that which everyone else knows.

21. Only God can raise the dead, and God can only raise the dead.

Epilogue

Albert Camus once said, 'The whole life of a person is the slow trek to recover the two or three simple images in whose presence his heart first moved.' The description 'first', I take it, is not temporal. The 'first' or primary movements of the heart are so called because they take place at a deeper level close to the origins of consciousness, the place of spirit, of creativity. They are one's essential, one's primary movements. They are much more 'you' than the multitude of your casual thoughts and wishes are.

I recall one such movement very clearly. In 1959 I was studying in Rome, and one day that summer I went on a picnic in the Campagna. After one of those orgies of pasta and red wine, features of a digestively stronger age, I wandered into a church where Vespers was just starting. It was the First Vespers of the Feast of the Sacred Heart. As I entered the church, I heard the familiar words, *Unus militum lancea latus eius aperuit, et continuo exivit sanguis et aqua* (One of the soldiers opened his side with a spear, and immediately there came forth blood and water). And I had what I can only describe as a sense of fullness of truth. Somehow, everything that was to be said about life and its renewing was in those words. Somehow *my* life, *my* destiny, was in those words.

Truth at that level is so different from truth as we normally seek it and dispute about it. It does not answer questions: it simply fills the heart. In its presence the heart moves. We know it as truth *in* the movement of the heart.

Thus although that image of the spear opening the side of Christ was destined to be the touchstone for decades of theologizing, it was fifteen years before I recalled it again. In the introduction to *The Crucified Is No Stranger*, I told this story and acknowledged this image as a mandate for exploring the mystery of the saving death.

Wherever I arrive conceptually in this exploration, the image is liable to pop up, always ahead of me, its peaceful fullness rebuking

119

the always partial findings of my thought. And now, as my thought has come so much further than it was when I wrote that introduction, the image is there again. And this time I can hold it in better focus.

What is it that, struck, yields the torrent, like the rock struck by Moses? Let me ask another question. What is the big discovery I am currently making in the theology of the cross? It pulls more together than any that I remember. It seems to answer *the* question: why did we *have* to be saved this way? The discovery is that Jesus awoke desire in his followers; that the desire he liberated is that infinite desire whose infinity we seldom sense directly; that this desire for life in its fullness chafes at life's limits and so moves in a mysterious harmony with death—'Death is the mother of beauty', as Wallace Stevens says; that this desire was altogether beyond their power to own, and so found its place-to-be *in* Jesus: the awakener of desire becomes its containing symbol. Thus the destruction, the dismantling, of the symbolic place of desire brought desire itself to the crisis that death will be for each of us. Living, they died, were carried beyond this world, knew what the dead know. And the focus of this spiritual enlargement, its agency, was the crucifixion of Jesus.

So we have our answer to the question, 'What is it that, struck, yields the torrent?' It is the heart of Jesus, the place of all desire, where our desire for limitless life is stored. And the heart knows, and the reason hardly understands, that the storehouse broken open yields the inexhaustible torrent.

In that deepest region of our mind, to which Camus refers, desire stores itself in symbol which is lifegiving precisely in dissolving itself. For psyche knows, better than we do, that we shall die. And psyche knows, better than we do, that death is indispensable to the fullness of life. And so psyche rehearses, in that deep clear region that is inaccessible to our muddying curiosity, the breaking-open of our life, of our desire, of our Christ, into the life that is undying, the Spirit that is all-sustaining.